the adventurous
VEGETARIAN

'If there were no such thing as eating, we should have to invent it to save man from despairing.' Dr Wilhelm Stekhel, The Depths of the Soul

the adventurous
VEGETARIAN

COLIN SPENCER

CASSELL

AN ADRIAN MORRIS BOOK

Cassell Publishers Limited
Artillery House, Artillery Row
London SW1P 1RT

Copyright © Adrian Morris Publishing Limited 1989
Text copyright © Colin Spencer 1989

First published 1989

Distributed in Australia by
Capricorn Link (Australia) Pty Ltd
PO Box 665, Lane Cove, NSW 20066

British Library Catalogue in Publication Data
Spencer, Colin
   The Adventurous Vegetarian
   1. Vegetarians, Food, Recipes
   I. Title
   641. 5'636

   ISBN 0-304-31808-6

Typeset by Pentacor Ltd, High Wycombe, Bucks
Colour separation by Bright Arts Ltd, Hong Kong
Printed in Singapore for Imago Publishing

Edited by Anne Johnson

THE ADVENTUROUS VEGETARIAN
was conceived and produced by
ADRIAN MORRIS PUBLISHING LIMITED
115J Cleveland Street
London W1P 5PN

CONTENTS

INTRODUCTION

'This world, after all our science and sciences, is still a miracle; wonderful, inscrutable, magical and more, to whosoever will think of it.' Thomas Carlyle

The collection of vegetarian recipes within these pages is culled from worldwide sources. Naturally, they reflect my own taste in food; hopefully, they also reflect both elegance and intensity of taste. I make no apologies for a choice which tends towards strong spices, pungent herbs and rich fusion of flavours. It was only the early vegetarian movement within Britain in the first part of this century that believed in food being somehow touched with moral earnestness, so that it tended towards the plain and worthy. The traditions of the rest of the world in their vegetable cooking are another story and, in a very small way, this book attempts to portray it.

If we could read the food of a country as we do its literature, it would tell us something similar. Food carries within it a complex stigma made up of a country's economy and geography, of its religion and history. It is a cultural holism which, in the past, we have dismissed as being somehow unworthy to contemplate seriously. It is one of the great ironies that food, which represents our survival, health and vigour, has so often been dismissed in the past as a subject worthy of serious study. Psychologically, the reason may be that it is precisely because it is so profoundly necessary to us

it feels too threatening a subject to peruse closely.

Whatever the cause, it is not difficult to see reflected in certain dishes the aspirations of various groups of people. The earnestness of British moral vegetarianism I have already mentioned, but consider also food used as weapon and punishment, as in the gruel of certain Victorian institutions and the vastly overcooked food, with little nutritional content, that was eaten in some public schools and, far worse, in prisons. Here the food, as dictated by the authorities, not only symbolises punishment but also has structured into its regime the jejune theory that unpleasantness is good for you.

Consider too the era of haute cuisine in France and other parts of western Europe. Think, for example, of the 25-course banquet which reflected not only status and wealth but also expansion and colonies, and communicated clear and powerful messages of the ruling elite towards the third world countries and the underlings who scampered about the huge halls and draughty kitchens serving, cooking and cleaning the dishes.

The eating of meat, of course, has always been a symbol of wealth and power, directly attached in its most primitive form to how many heads of cattle you can, as a farmer or herdsman, afford to

slaughter. Meat eating in all societies, except for those with religious taboos against it, has carried within it this cultural meaning, even when the household is urban and poor and members of it have never even seen a live cow or a slaughterhouse. A haunch of meat was always eaten, if possible, on Sundays and feast days, and certainly as a form of celebration. Partly because of this, worldwide vegetarian cooking is often associated with the poor, the lower classes and the peasants. One of the great ironies of food is that the rich, in most cases, give themselves terminal illnesses through over-eating and the consumption of too many fats and sugars. The poor, on the other hand, if they can actually consume enough food, eat on the whole a nutritionally well-balanced diet.

The vegetarian dishes of the world, therefore, tend to be not only those of the poorest elements of society, but also the healthiest. They are often street food and certainly everyday dishes, with no pretension to greatness. This, for me, makes vegetarian food supremely fascinating. I believe that the most striking combinations of ingredients and flavours are born out of necessity, because the palate needs interest to sustain digestion.

Hence it follows that innovations in food are created by the lower classes and then taken up by the rest of society. The plain food of the lower classes has always been a form of gruel or porridge made from grains, whether wheat, corn, oats or rice, depending on the grain that thrives in that particular country. This porridge is generally moistened and made more interesting by what is mixed with it. Thus, in eastern Europe, buckwheat is a staple, and the porridge is eaten with butter, salt and sometimes egg. In Rumania, the porridge is Mamaliga, which is made from maize eaten with onions; in Italy, the cornmeal becomes polenta; while in America, poor southerners are eating it as hominy grits. The same grain, further south in Mexico, is made into tortillas, or tamales or tacos—all much the same flat bread used to wrap around food, while the filling would be heavily spiced with chillies, sweet peppers, garlic and onion. The rice porridge of India is eaten with yoghurt, or with mung beans and spinach; and the congee of China is flavoured with soy and a whole variety of spices; and in Tibet, their porridge (tsampa) is made from barley and mixed with hot tea and rank butter.

In poor families, dishes are created from what is at hand. There are, for example, one-pot meals, which need long, slow cooking over the fire while the

family are out in the fields. One-pot dishes are often made from scraps of meat or fish, but many of them, such as the French cassoulet and pot au feu, the Brazilian feijouda and the tagines of north Africa, began life as vegetables and beans. And then there are the many grain dishes, consisting of the basic grain and a collection of foods gathered or killed on the day. One of the most famous dishes in the world, the paella of Spain, began in the rice-growing areas of river deltas along the coast and was flavoured with the herbs and beans growing on the banks of fields, while protein came from eels and rabbits. You did not shoot your own hens when you needed the eggs!

I have tried in each chapter to choose only one dish from a country which I have either especially liked, tasted or cooked, or which has seemed highly characteristic in its origin. But when there is more than one, it is that the dishes are so singular that they begged for inclusion.

In culinary terms, the world can be crudely divided up into eight sections, and I have divided the world roughly thus:

1. Western Europe. This includes, of course, France which in its classical cuisine has many great vegetarian dishes, even though in that country the title vegetarian appears still to be a dirty word. There are only a few recipes from northern Europe, for the best of their cooking revolves around salted and smoked fish.

2. The northern Mediterranean. This includes Spain, Italy and Greece, which are all important and singular in culinary terms.

3. Eastern Europe, the Balkans, Poland and Russia. They all share a cuisine which has much in common. There is, sadly, little pure vegetarian cooking in it, but there are a few dishes which are memorable and must be included, such as blinis, borscht and bagels, and an interesting use of horseradish, paprika, yoghurt and soured cream. This is a cuisine that calls up yeasty breads and caraway seeds, cabbage and thick winter stews.

4. The Middle East, Turkey and the Arab countries, Egypt and parts of north Africa. This area includes the southern Mediterranean, which has a similar cooking based on grains such as semolina (couscous), buckwheat and bulgar as well as rice, and on spices such as coriander and cumin.

Flavours are redolent with garlic, lemons and limes, aubergines and tomatoes. Claudia Roden has made the cooking of this huge and varied area famous, and I am always in her debt.

5. Black Africa. This is a cuisine which influenced the Caribbean and Cajun cooking, but it is an area of the world with which I am still largely unfamiliar. What I have tasted is sensational enough, though, so I have included the dishes I know.

6. India and, most particularly, southern India where Hinduism flourishes. This area is the most significant in the world for its range of great and varied vegetarian dishes. It includes Kerala, with its use of thin pancakes and coconut to flavour curries, Madras, with its fiery hot stews, and the cinnamon sweet curries of the Moghuls of Hyderabad.

7. The Far East. This area, highly important in world cuisine, comprises China and the whole of south-east Asia, from Thailand to Japan. Oddly enough, the food is not renowned for pure vegetarian dishes, as many of the vegetable recipes are often cooked in chicken or fish stock, and fish sauce (nuoc-nam in Vietnam, nam pla in Thailand) is used extensively to flavour the plainest dish of rice and vegetables. But this area is also the home of tofu or bean curd, and wherever Hindu or Buddhist cultures have influenced society, vegetarianism flourishes in some form or other. The recipes from this area are, I must admit, some of my own favourites.

8. The Americas. The most excellent cooking in the whole of this vast continent comes from the Caribbean and Mexico, where there is a wonderful fusion in the former of Spain, Africa, India and France, and a huge reliance in the latter on some of my favourite flavours, including sweetcorn, chillies, garlic, peppers and avocado. Neither cuisine is known for its vegetarian dishes, but I have chosen a few which I think are highly memorable.

I have placed the recipes in each chapter in order, beginning with western Europe, the Mediterranean, eastern Europe and the Middle East; then continuing with Africa, India, the Far East and concluding with the Americas.

I hope that the reader will find much to stimulate the mind within these pages as well as enchanting the palate.

SMALL BEGINNINGS

'The truth is that the beginning of anything and its end are alike touching.'
Yoshida Kenko, Life Frailing and Fleeting

This chapter is about street food or, as some books refer to it, finger food: food we eat on the move, or food to eat at a party.

I believe that nowhere so clearly does a country show its character as in its cooking on the street. Difficult, you might think, to see much character in a frankfurter stuffed in the pale dry dough of a bun, but perhaps this is the point I am making: when street food is taken over by large monopolies, its individual character is destroyed.

To see what I mean, you have to go East, to Singapore, where so many traditions and cultures meet. The open-air street stalls here might be serving an Indian curry with nan and chutney on a banana leaf; or you can eat Indonesian, Malay, Korean or Thai; or you can choose among Chinese styles, Peking and Szechuan, Canton, Shanghai, Hunan, Hokkien or Hakka, where the favourite dish is Yong Tau Foo or stuffed bean curd. On the streets, you may eat Hokkien fried noodles; an Indian pancake called Murtabah; the wonderful Chinese cake, Chye Tow Kway, made from the white daikon radish; or a Popiah, which is a thin pancake smeared with chilli sauce and piled high with bean sprouts, turnip, nuts, cucumber and more chilli. You can wash your meal down with soya milk, Kam Chia (sugar cane water) or Ya Chui (coconut water), and it will all cost the equivalent of less than £1.

The recipes I have chosen here range from those cheese pastries called Kremythopittas, which you buy warm in the streets of Athens and versions of which appear all over the Middle East and even as far afield as the island of Malta (obviously the knights took such a favoured morsel with them from Rhodes); to chips made from plantain, which derive from Africa and appear too in India, where they are flavoured with turmeric.

Pizzette col Pomodoro Crudo e Basilico

ITALY

Small pizzas with raw tomato and basil

You can find pizzettes in virtually any street in Italy, but these are ones to be made at home when the first basil leaves of the season appear.

Pizza dough:
300 g (11 oz) strong unbleached flour
1 teaspoon sea salt
½ teaspoon yeast granules
175 ml (6 fl oz) tepid water
2 tablespoons olive oil
Topping:
1½ fresh tomatoes
3 tablespoons olive oil
sea salt and freshly ground black pepper
handful of basil leaves

First make the pizza dough. Mix all the dried ingredients together, then add the water and oil. Mix thoroughly and knead. Leave to rise in a warm place for 1 hour, or in a cool place for several hours. Then punch out the air and divide into six or eight portions. Roll into balls and flatten each one to form a circle. Lay on a non-stick baking tray and leave to prove for 15 minutes.

Now prepare the topping. Slice the tomatoes thinly, lay on the pizzette and dribble olive oil over each one. Season with salt and pepper, and bake in a preheated hot oven, at 220°C (425°F), Gas Mark 7, for 15 minutes. Dribble more oil over the top and sprinkle with basil leaves.

Makes 6 to 8

Tapenade
FRANCE
Olive spread

Made from black olives, capers, anchovies and garlic, tapenade comes from that part of France where black olives ripen in the sun and add their rich, tangy flavour to so many dishes. This simplified vegetarian version of tapenade is spread on French bread so that the bread soaks up the flavours. This olive bread is good cut up in small pieces and used instead of croûtons in a salad.

120 g (4 oz) stoned black olives
3 cloves garlic, crushed
2 tablespoons capers
3 tablespoons olive oil
1 French loaf
olives or capers to garnish

Place the olives, garlic, capers and olive oil in an electric blender or food processor and liquidise to a purée.

Slice the loaf of bread and toast on one side only. Spread the untoasted side with the tapenade and place under the grill until hot and bubbly. Garnish each slice with either half a black olive or a few capers.

Serves 4 to 6

Kremythopittas
GREECE
Small cheese and onion pastries

The smell of cheese and buttered pastry alerts you to the stall selling these delicious pastries, which you will find all over Greece and its islands. They are easy to make at home and a fine party food.

2 packets of feta cheese
2 onions, grated
1 egg, beaten
freshly ground black pepper
zest of 1 lemon
12 sheets of filo pastry
50 g (2 oz) melted butter
2 tablespoons sesame seeds

Crumble the feta in a bowl. Add the grated onions, egg, pepper and lemon zest, and mix thoroughly.

Cut the sheets of filo pastry in half lengthways and spread a thin layer of the cheese and onion mixture over each sheet to 1 cm (½ inch) of the border. Using a pastry brush, paint the border with a little melted butter. Then carefully roll the filo away from you, tucking in the sides as you go. Lay each pastry on a non-stick baking sheet, paint with melted butter and sprinkle with sesame seeds.

Bake in a preheated hot oven at 220°C (425°F), Gas Mark 7 for 15 minutes or until puffed up and golden brown.

Serves 4 to 6

Feta cheese *A Greek cheese made from goat's or sheep's milk, which is white, crumbly and moist. It comes in brine and varies in saltiness.*

Saganaki
CYPRUS
Fried haloumi cheese

Fried haloumi makes an excellent appetiser with any drink from ouzo to a dry martini. Indeed, I have even enjoyed it with champagne. A simpler version is to grill the slices of cheese rather than frying them with oregano as they are here.

3 tablespoons olive oil
1 tablespoon dried oregano
1 tablespoon dried thyme
150 g (5 oz) Cypriot haloumi cheese,
cut in 5mm (¼ inch) slices
1 lemon, quartered, to garnish

Heat the oil in a pan and throw in the herbs. Cook for a few seconds, then place the cheese slices in the hot oil, not allowing them to touch. Fry quickly for 1 minute so that the cheese becomes crisp and brown, then turn over and cook the other side.

Drain on absorbent paper and serve with the lemon sliced into quarters.

Serves 4 to 6

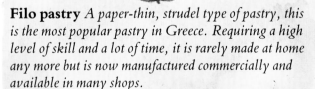

Filo pastry *A paper-thin, strudel type of pastry, this is the most popular pastry in Greece. Requiring a high level of skill and a lot of time, it is rarely made at home any more but is now manufactured commercially and available in many shops.*
Haloumi cheese *Creamy white ewe's cheese from Cyprus. It can be bought in some supermarkets and all specialist Greek and Cypriot stores.*

Empanadillas de Espinaca
SPAIN
Spinach turnovers

These small pastry turnovers are often served as part of a selection of appetisers, or tapas. The pine nuts in the filling make it especially good and are reminiscent of other recipes from the Middle East.

450 g (1 lb) spinach
25 g (1 oz) butter
3 tablespoons olive oil
3 tablespoons pine nuts, chopped
5 cloves garlic, crushed
3 tablespoons raisins, soaked in warm water for 3 minutes,
then drained and chopped
sea salt and freshly ground black pepper
225 g (8 oz) frozen puff pastry, thawed
1 egg, beaten

Cook the spinach with the butter over a low flame. When it has reduced to a third of its volume, allow to cool, then drain and chop coarsely.

Heat the olive oil and throw in the pine nuts with the garlic and raisins. Cook for a moment, just to brown the nuts, then mix with the spinach and season with salt and pepper.

Roll out the pastry to about an eighth of its thickness. Cut into triangles about 7.5 cm (3 inches) in length. Place a little of the spinach mixture over one half of the triangle, leaving a 5 mm (¼ inch) border, moisten the edges with beaten egg, then fold over and press the edges together. Place on a baking tray, paint the tops with more egg and bake in a preheated hot oven, at 220°C (425°F), Gas Mark 7, for 15 minutes or until risen and golden brown.

Serves 4 to 6

Halushki
RUSSIA
Potato dumplings

These are small vegetable dumplings from eastern Europe, a version of which you will find in many countries. The insides are often tinged with pink if a hot or sweet paprika has been added.

750 g (1½ lb) potatoes, boiled and mashed
1 tablespoon caraway seeds
1 teaspoon sea salt
3 tablespoons plain flour
1 large egg
To fry:
flour, beaten egg and breadcrumbs
vegetable oil, such as olive, corn or sunflower

Mix the mashed potatoes with the caraway seeds, salt, flour and egg. Knead together to make a pliable dough. Roll small pieces of dough, the size of walnuts, into balls and dip into the flour, then the beaten egg and finally the breadcrumbs before frying in hot oil. Fry until brown and crisp on all sides. Serve with a mixture of chopped chives and sour cream.

Serves 4 to 6

Gram flour, *sometimes known as besan flour, is made from ground chick peas. It has a good flavour and creamy texture, and is much used in Indian cooking to coat foods prior to frying them. It is also used in soups and sauces. It is unrefined, so it will always need sifting before use to prevent lumps.*

Eggah bi Konsa
EGYPT
Small courgette omelettes

I believe the flavour of courgettes to be best when the vegetable is either raw or only just cooked. These are very simple to make and taste heavenly. They are extremely light because of the gram or chick pea flour, which barely holds them together.

3–4 medium courgettes
sea salt and freshly ground black pepper
1 tablespoon gram flour, sifted
2 tablespoons milk
4 eggs, beaten
generous handful of parsley, finely chopped
oil for frying

Grate the courgettes into a colander, sprinkle with salt and leave for 1 hour. Mix the gram flour with the milk and make a thick paste, then beat in the eggs. Season with pepper. Squeeze the courgettes dry and add to the egg mixture, along with the parsley. Mix thoroughly.

Use a small drop of oil in a pan and add a tablespoon of the egg mixture to make a small omelette. Cook briefly on both sides. Several omelettes can be cooked at once—this mixture makes about eight.

Serves 4 to 6

Aubergine Slices with Garlic
MIDDLE EAST

The aubergine is one of the most popular vegetables in the Middle East and there are countless recipes which use it, both alone and with other vegetables. Not all aubergine recipes tell you to slice and salt the vegetable and then to leave it for an hour to drain but I believe it is essential, both to get rid of some of the bitter juices and also to stop it soaking up so much oil in the cooking that it becomes unpalatable. There are many recipes for aubergine slices but, because of my fondness for garlic, this is one of my favourites.

2 medium aubergines
sea salt
olive oil
4–6 cloves garlic, thinly sliced
freshly ground black pepper
lemon wedges

Cut the aubergines across in 5 mm (¼ inch) slices, sprinkle with a little salt, and leave in a colander for 1 hour. Then wash the salt away and pat dry.

Heat plenty of olive oil in a pan and fry the slices for a few minutes on each side until brown and crisp. When all the aubergine is cooked, throw the thinly sliced garlic into the pan and fry briefly so that it is also golden brown.

Sprinkle the garlic over the aubergine, grind the peppermill over them and serve with wedges of lemon so that people can squeeze their own.

Serves 4 to 6

Makote
AFRICA
Plantain chips

Both plantains and sweet potatoes are excellent for making chips, and cook much more quickly than potatoes. Luckily, you can now buy these vegetables in many of our own street markets and big stores. This is good street food in many parts of the world, including Africa, the West Indies, South America and India.

2 medium plantains
corn oil for frying
sea salt and freshly ground black pepper

Peel the plantains and, if they are too large, halve or quarter them, then slice them across in 1 cm (½ inch) chunks. Heat the oil and fry for a few minutes until golden brown, then drain and sprinkle with salt and pepper.

Serves 4 to 6

Plantains *These are a variety of banana used for cooking. They are larger than other bananas, usually green in colour, and are used in many Caribbean and African dishes. They are not suitable for eating raw.*

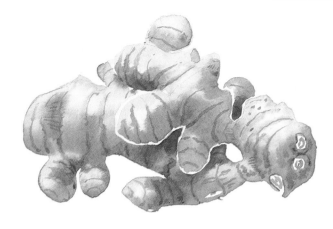

Chilla
INDIA
Chick pea pancakes

These small fiery pancakes are eaten for breakfast in India and would certainly be more efficient at waking you up than an alarm clock. They are best, perhaps, eaten here with cool yoghurt as part of a first course.

120 g (4 oz) gram flour, sifted (see page 16)
300 ml (½ pint) water
1 tablespoon root ginger, grated
2 green chillies, seeded and thinly sliced
2 red chillies, seeded and thinly sliced
2 tablespoons sesame oil
1 teaspoon sea salt
sunflower oil for frying

Mix all the ingredients together thoroughly, except the sunflower oil, and beat well. An electric blender or food processor will do the job most efficiently.

Heat the sunflower oil in a pan and pour in a tablespoon of the batter to make small pancakes. Several can be cooked at once, but do not let them run into each other. Fry briefly on both sides. Keep warm until the whole batch is done.

Serves 4 to 6

Potato Balls
TANZANIA

It was the Asians settling in East Africa that brought the use of coconut to these countries, and both the milk and the flesh are frequently used in cooking. There are recipes all over the world for potato balls but this is the only one I know which uses chilli or cayenne pepper with coconut. I think it is particularly delicious.

1 kg (2 lb) potatoes, peeled, cooked and mashed
zest and juice of 2 limes
½ teaspoon cayenne pepper
½ teaspoon sea salt
50 g (2 oz) creamed coconut, grated
120 g (4 oz) gram flour, sifted (see page 16)
corn or sunflower oil for frying

Mix the potatoes with the lime zest and juice, cayenne pepper, salt and coconut. Add 50 g (2 oz) of the gram flour and knead into a dough. Make small cakes or balls, roll them in the rest of the flour and fry in hot oil until crisp and brown.

Serves 4 to 6

Tempura Vegetables
JAPAN

This is one of the most popular dishes in Japan and, if the vegetables are chosen for their contrasting colours and cut stylishly, it is also one of the most attractive. The two things to remember are to ensure that the batter is light enough and that the vegetables are not overcooked.

few sprigs of broccoli
2 small carrots, thinly sliced
2 small courgettes, thinly sliced
corn oil for frying
Batter:
120 g (4 oz) plain flour, sifted
sea salt
150 ml (¼ pint) water
1 egg white, beaten

Do not peel the vegetables, but slice them thinly into strips.

To make the batter, mix the seasoned flour with the water to make a thin goo, then fold in the stiffened egg white. Use at once. Dip the vegetables in the batter, coating them on all sides. Heat the oil in a wok and deep fry, turning the vegetables over so that they are crisp on the outside but still al dente inside.

Serves 4 to 6

Tea Eggs
CHINA

These look so stunning with their antique marbling that I forgive them the fact that the process of cooking tends to make the whites slightly rubbery. However, they are considered a delicacy in the Far East and are worth making because they look so good on the table. They can be used to garnish dishes of noodles and stir-fried vegetables.

12 eggs
600 ml (1 pint) strong tea

Place the eggs in a pan of cold water and bring to the boil, then cover, turn the heat off and leave for 10 minutes. The eggs will now be perfectly cooked.

Next, crack the shell gently with a spoon to form hairline cracks all over the surface. Place these eggs in the tea and simmer for 20 minutes. Leave to cool and then shell the eggs. They should be marbled with the colour of the tea.

Makes 12

Soya Eggs
THAILAND

Like Tea Eggs, these look attractive used either as a garnish or alone as an appetiser. So often in the Far East, you will find food that is served more for its aesthetic impact than its flavour. Here the flavour is strong and pleasant, but these eggs can suffer from the same problem of slightly rubbery whites as the Tea Eggs.

4–6 hard-boiled eggs
2 tablespoons corn oil
4 cloves garlic, crushed
85 ml (3 fl oz) soy sauce
2 tablespoons soft brown sugar

Peel the eggs and then, with a sharp knife, score them lightly lengthways about four times on each side. Heat the oil and fry the garlic in it gently for a moment, then add the soy and sugar. Cook until the sugar has dissolved, then place the eggs in the sauce and simmer, turning the eggs several times so that they absorb the colour and flavour of the soy. Eat warm or cold.

Makes 4 to 6

Sweetcorn Fritters
AMERICA

All recipes using corn kernels and maize flour, so popular in America, come originally from Mexico and the deep South. These fritters are a traditional accompaniment to Chicken Maryland, though they are just as commonly eaten as appetisers and very good they are too. It is now possible to buy frozen sweetcorn kernels without any additives, including sugar, and this is a great help for dishes such as this; before that, you had to cut the kernels from the cob, either before or after cooking, which was a terrible chore.

1 egg
50 g (2 oz) plain flour, sifted
4 tablespoons milk
3 tablespoons corn kernels
½ teaspoon sea salt
freshly ground black pepper
sunflower or corn oil for frying

Add the egg to the flour to make a smooth paste, then beat in the milk. Add the corn kernels and seasonings. Mix thoroughly.

Drop spoonfuls of the mixture into hot oil and fry until crisp and golden. Drain on absorbent paper.

Serves 4 to 6

Banana Chips
JAMAICA

These delicious chips, made from green bananas, are hugely popular with children. This is street food at its simplest and best.

4 or 5 green bananas
salt
sunflower oil for frying

Peel the bananas, slice them into fairly thin discs and leave in salted water for 15 minutes. Dry thoroughly.

Fry in hot sunflower oil until they are crisp. Drain on absorbent paper, sprinkle with salt and serve, or store in an airtight jar.

Serves 4 to 6

23

SOUPS, SUMMER AND WINTER

'I declare that a meal prepared by a person who loves you will do more good than any average cooking, and on the other side of it a person who dislikes you is bound to get that dislike into your food, without intending to.' Luther Burbank, The Harvest of the Years

It would not be difficult to write a whole book of world soups, so good are a multitude of recipes. These are only a modest beginning to such an enterprise.

It is also an interesting fact that the best soups tend to come from the coldest parts of the world, where they are meant to be filling and warming: not so much to entice and beguile the palate, as in the Far East, as to form part of the main substance of the meal. I have included two such soups from Ireland and Finland, both made from the cheapest of ingredients (potatoes and cabbage), but not to be despised for that as they are marvellously warming on a cold winter's day.

This section begins with cool soups for summer and I have tried to pick examples which are not obvious. There is no Spanish gazpacho here— which is very overrated—but a sensational almond and garlic soup. There is also a cold Jamaican soup of avocado flavoured with lime, which might strike us as sophisticated but which is glaringly obvious to them as they are surrounded by the ingredients.

Soups from the Far East which satisfy the stomach or the palate are not that plentiful, for they see soups as having the rather different purpose of refreshing the palate. I chose Hot Pepper Soup from China because it has three of my favourite ingredients—salted black beans, chillies and ginger—and its effect on the palate is vastly stimulating. The soup from Thailand is a quieter affair: there are few recipes here which include tofu (so many vegetarian books depend on it too much) but this soup, flavoured with lemon grass, lime and ginger, works beautifully.

A word on vegetable stock: I am delighted to say that there are now some excellent vegetable stock cubes available in most shops, where the flavour is not sullied by artifice or the blood of baby chickens. They are infinitely superior to the carnivorous version of stock cubes, which are made from the scraps and bones of carcasses. Use 1 or 2 stock cubes to 600 ml (1 pint) of water, 3 for 1.2 litres (2 pints), but watch how salty the stock is or, better still, use salt-free cubes which are also widely available. There are also vegetable bouillon powders which are useful to add to the stock if you want to increase its intensity. When you have a thin or clear soup, as in some of the Eastern recipes, you need a richly flavoured liquor.

Cool Soups

Suppe aus die Kirsche	GERMANY	27
Danish Apple Soup	SCANDINAVIA	28
Ajo Blanco de Málaga	SPAIN	28
Tarator	BULGARIA	29
Avocado and Lime Soup	JAMAICA	29

Hot Soups

Potato and Fresh Herb Soup	IRELAND	30
Minestrone	ITALY	30
Soupe à l'Ail	FRANCE	32
Cabbage and Chestnut Soup	FINLAND	32
Borscht	RUSSIA	33
Onion Soup	PERSIA	33
Clear Mushroom and Mangetout Soup	JAPAN	35
Cantonese Hot Pepper Bean Soup	CHINA	36
Ginger and Bean Curd Soup	THAILAND	36
Boston Mushroom Soup	AMERICA	37
Vegetable Soup with Chocolate	MEXICO	37

Suppe aus die Kirsche
GERMANY
Cherry soup

We generally associate cherry soup with Hungary, but this German version is made with red wine and is stronger and less fruity than the Balkan version. It is a marvellous beginning to a meal on a hot summer's evening.

450 g (1 lb) cherries, stoned
600 ml (1 pint) red wine
600 ml (1 pint) water
juice and zest of 2 oranges
soured cream or smetana to garnish

Heat the cherries with the rest of the ingredients and simmer for 15 minutes. Leave to cool.

Blend and either chill for a few hours, or reheat gently. Serve with a spoonful of soured cream or smetana.

Serves 4 to 6

Smetana *A kind of low-fat soured cream which can be used as a healthier alternative to cream or soured cream in savoury dishes. It is lower in fat because it is made of a combination of skimmed milk and cream.*

Danish Apple Soup
SCANDINAVIA

This recipe has much nostalgia for me. My great-grandmother, who was Danish, brought it over to England at the end of the nineteenth century and, when I was a child, it was made for me by her daughter, my own grandmother. Though it was not until the end of the Second World War that it was made with blue cheese, I suspect that blue cheese may in any case have been too strong for my palate then. Now I believe that the soup needs that flavour, but do buy a good farmhouse blue.

50 g (2 oz) butter
450 g (1 lb) Cox's or Newton Pippin apples,
peeled, cored and chopped
1.2 litres (2 pints) vegetable stock
juice and zest of 1 lemon
8 tablespoons dry white wine
50 g (2 oz) creamy blue cheese
salt and freshly ground black pepper
To garnish:
1 Cox's or Newton Pippin apple, cored but not peeled
few sprigs of chervil

Melt 40 g (1½ oz) of the butter in a pan. Add the apples and cook for 2 minutes before adding the stock, lemon juice and zest, and wine. Simmer gently for about 20 minutes.

Remove from the heat and break up the apple pieces with a whisk. Add the cheese and reheat gently, allowing the cheese to melt. Season to taste.

Slice the cored apples and fry the rings in the remaining butter until soft. Use to garnish the soup, and top with sprigs of chervil.

Serves 4 to 6

Ajo Blanco de Málaga
SPAIN
Almond soup

This soup is one of my favourites. It looks wonderfully creamy from the ground almonds which blend beautifully with the garlic.

1 head of garlic (12–15 cloves)
85 ml (3 fl oz) olive oil
300 ml (½ pint) water
120 g (4 oz) almonds, blanched
350 g (12 oz) white bread, soaked in water
2 eggs, beaten
85 ml (3 fl oz) dry sherry
1 teaspoon sea salt
freshly ground white pepper to taste
900 ml (1½ pints) vegetable stock
To garnish:
white grapes
slices of apple

Peel the cloves of garlic. Heat the olive oil in a pan and soften the garlic slightly, then add water and simmer gently for 30 minutes. Allow to cool.

Meanwhile, drain the almonds, add these to the garlic stock, and liquidise to a purée in a food processor. Squeeze the moisture out of the bread, add to the mixture with the rest of the ingredients, and blend again.

Chill for a few hours. Serve cold garnished with white grapes and slices of apple.

Serves 4 to 6

Tarator
BULGARIA

This recipe is not unlike the Greek jajiki, though this has the addition of pine kernels and is very much a cool soup rather than a dip. Yoghurt is always highly refreshing in hot weather, which is why it is used so often in Indian cuisine.

1 cucumber, grated
1 teaspoon sea salt
900 ml (1½ pints) natural yoghurt
3 cloves garlic, crushed
50 g (2 oz) walnuts
50 g (2 oz) pine kernels
3 tablespoons chopped mint

Sprinkle the cucumber with salt and leave for 1 hour, then stir in the yoghurt and garlic. Crush the walnuts and pine kernels in a blender, and add these to the soup.

Chill the soup for a few hours. Add the chopped mint just before serving.

Serves 4 to 6

Avocado and Lime Soup
JAMAICA

Ripe avocados make the most beautifully coloured soups of all, and the lime zest in this recipe makes a huge difference to the flavour.

3 ripe avocado pears
zest and juice of 3 limes
1.2 litres (2 pints) vegetable stock
sea salt and freshly ground black pepper
2–3 spring onions, finely sliced, to garnish

Take the flesh from the avocados and place in a liquidiser with the lime zest and juice. Add the vegetable stock to make a smooth purée.

Season to taste with salt and pepper. Serve cold and garnish with finely sliced spring onions.

Serves 4 to 6

Potato and Fresh Herb Soup
IRELAND

I try to taste this soup every time I visit Ireland, though sadly the simplest dishes are not always the easiest to find. Any fresh herbs can be added to the soup at the end instead of parsley and chives, such as dill, chervil and basil. Potatoes, are marvellous at soaking up flavours.

1.5 litres (2½ pints) water
large sprig of rosemary
3 bay leaves
25 g (1 oz) butter
450 g (1 lb) potatoes, peeled and diced
1 large onion, diced
generous bunch of parsley, finely chopped
bunch of chives, finely chopped
sea salt and freshly ground black pepper
150 ml (¼ pint) single cream

Bring the water to the boil and simmer the rosemary and bay leaves for 10 minutes. Discard the herbs.

Melt the butter in a saucepan and add the diced potatoes and onion. Stir for a moment or two, then add the water in which the herbs have been infusing. Simmer for 20 minutes, then add the parsley, chives and seasonings. Allow to cool, then blend and reheat gently, adding the cream.

Serves 4 to 6

Minestrone
ITALY

I fear this great soup has acquired a name for mediocrity, both because it appears so often on the menus of unenterprising restaurants and because the canning industry has done little to help it to be respected. All too often, this soup is a result of leftovers in the kitchen chucked together in a saucepan and flavoured inadequately with a weak stock. If you add pesto (see page 124) to it at the table, you will have something approaching another great soup, a near cousin, soupe au pistou, from nearby Geneva.

85 ml (3 fl oz) olive oil
3 cloves garlic, crushed
1 onion, thinly sliced
1 carrot, thinly sliced
1 stick celery, thinly sliced
1 green pepper, cored, seeded and thinly sliced
¼ white cabbage, shredded
225 g (8 oz) potatoes, peeled and diced
225 g (8 oz) courgettes, thinly sliced
2.75 litres (5 pints) water
50 g (2 oz) broken spaghetti or vermicelli
120 g (4 oz) cooked cannelloni beans
sea salt and freshly ground black pepper
50 g (2 oz) Parmesan cheese, freshly grated

Heat the olive oil in a large pan and throw in the garlic and all the vegetables. Stir well and cook for a few moments, then add the water. Bring to the boil and simmer for 30 minutes.

Now add the broken pasta and beans, and cook for a further 10 minutes. Season with salt and pepper, and sprinkle with Parmesan just before serving.

Serves 10

Soupe à l'Ail
FRANCE
Garlic soup

There are hundreds of recipes for garlic soup, especially from the Iberian peninsular and France. This is one of the simplest. Taste it and see how good it can be. Then experiment with a little touch of saffron, which is the only possible improvement.

3 heads of garlic
85 ml (3 fl oz) olive oil
sea salt and freshly ground black pepper
1.2 litres (2 pints) vegetable stock
2 egg yolks
3 tablespoons chopped parsley

Blanch the cloves of garlic so that they peel easily. Heat the olive oil and throw the peeled garlic into it with the seasonings. Fry gently for 5 minutes. Add the vegetable stock and simmer for 20 minutes. Leave to cool.

Blend, then reheat gently. Add a little hot soup to the egg yolks in a mixing bowl, stir and pour back into the soup. Stir and continue to reheat until slightly thickened. Sprinkle with chopped parsley just before serving.

Serves 4 to 6

Cabbage and Chestnut Soup
FINLAND

Chestnuts and cabbage are natural partners. This soup is extra good if you wash it down with an eau de vie or a neat, well-iced vodka.

120 g (4 oz) dried chestnuts, soaked
1.5 litres (2½ pints) water
50 g (2 oz) butter
1 medium white cabbage
5 cloves garlic, crushed
1 large onion, sliced
sea salt and freshly ground black pepper
generous bunch of parsley, finely chopped

Simmer the chestnuts in half the water for 1 hour. Pick out the bits of outer skin that stay in the crevices and break up the nuts.

Melt the butter and cook the cabbage, garlic and onion until soft, then add the rest of the water and seasonings. Simmer for 15 minutes.

Blend the chestnuts to a purée in their liquor and add to the soup. Reheat gently, stirring in the parsley before serving.

Serves 4 to 6

Borscht
RUSSIA

I cannot resist including this soup, probably the most famous of all Russian dishes. If it is well made and the beetroots are freshly bought soon after they have been dug out of the earth, both the flavour and the colour are sublime. It also makes, of course, a marvellous cold soup.

750 g (1½ lb) raw beetroots, peeled and diced
1 small cabbage, sliced
5 cloves garlic, crushed
2 onions, sliced
1.5 litres (2½ pints) water
sea salt and freshly ground black pepper
150 ml (¼ pint) soured cream

Put all the vegetables in a large pan and add the water. Bring to the boil and simmer for 2 hours.

Liquidise the soup in a blender and season with salt and pepper. Reheat gently and serve with the soured cream.

Serves 4 to 6

Onion Soup
IRAN

We are familiar with the French classic onion soup but this one from the Middle East is, I believe, preferable. The French soup needs long slow cooking to caramelise the onions. This one takes its colour from the spices and if, like me, you like the flavour of asofoetida, a spice which is a large root indigenous to this part of the world, then you will enjoy the flavour.

3 tablespoons olive oil
4 large onions, sliced
1 tablespoon asofoetida
1 tablespoon turmeric 1 teaspoon cinnamon
2 tablespoons plain flour, sifted
1.5 litres (2½ pints) vegetable stock
zest and juice of 1 lemon
sea salt and freshly ground black pepper
2 egg yolks, beaten
generous handful of mint, chopped

Heat the oil in a large pan and add the onions and spices. Fry gently until soft, then add the flour. Cook for a moment before adding the stock, lemon zest and juice. Simmer for 10 minutes and season.

Add some hot soup to the beaten eggs, stir until it thickens slightly, then return to the rest of the soup. Reheat gently and sprinkle with chopped mint.

Serves 4 to 6

Asofoetida *This is the dried gum exuded from the living rhizome of of a plant called Ferula, which grows in India, Afghanistan and Iran. Sold in lump or powder form, it has a subtle onion-like aroma.*

Clear Mushroom and Mangetout Soup
JAPAN

This clear soup is typical of many Far Eastern soups, where the vegetables are hardly cooked but float in a strong clear stock. If you need the soup to taste stronger, dissolve a stock cube in the mushroom soaking water.

50 g (2 oz) dried mushrooms or fungi
600 ml (1 pint) water
2 tablespoons sesame oil
120 g (4 oz) mangetout peas
50 g (2 oz) wholewheat noodles
25 g (1 oz) ginger, grated
3 tablespoons light soy sauce
85 ml (3 fl oz) dry sherry

Soak the mushrooms in the water for a few hours. Drain and reserve the water. Slice the mushrooms into strips, heat the sesame oil and fry them gently for a few minutes.

Slice the mangetout peas diagonally and steam them for 2–3 minutes. Cook the noodles so that they are tender but al dente. Pour the mushroom soaking water over the mushrooms, adding all the other ingredients. Reheat gently. If you need more liquid, you can increase the volume with a little vegetable stock.

Serves 4 to 6

Cantonese Hot Pepper Bean Soup
CHINA

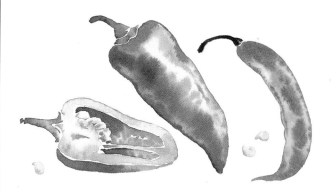

Salted black beans are used extensively in China. This is a variation on many Chinese soups using ginger, chillies and beans.

1 head of garlic
85 ml (3 fl oz) sesame oil
25 g (1 oz) ginger root, peeled and grated
1.2 litres (2 pints) vegetable stock
3 green chillies, seeded and chopped
3 red chillies, seeded and chopped
8 g (¼ oz) salted black beans
freshly ground szechuan pepper

Blanch the cloves of garlic so that they peel easily. Heat the sesame oil and sauté the garlic and ginger for a few minutes, then add some of the stock and blend to a purée. Add the chillies, beans, szechuan pepper and remaining stock. Simmer for 10 minutes.

Serves 4 to 6

Ginger and Bean Curd Soup
THAILAND

This soup is intended, in Thailand, to be eaten as part of the main course, so it is meant to be refreshing rather than sustaining.

50 g (2 oz) tofu
600 ml (1 pint) water
25 g (1 oz) ginger, peeled and grated
zest and juice of 2 limes
2 spears lemon grass
120 g (4 oz) frozen petits pois
3 tablespoons light soy sauce
600 ml (1 pint) vegetable stock

Slice the tofu thinly, then cut into small dice. Blanch in the water and leave for 15 minutes. Drain, reserving the water. Use this to cook the ginger and lime zest, simmering for 15 minutes. Pour through a sieve, reserving the liquor but discarding the ginger and lime.

Cook the lemon grass and petits pois in the reserved water. Then add the lime juice, bean curd, soy and stock. Simmer for 5 minutes.

Serves 4 to 6

Lemon grass *Several species of grass, widely used in south-east Asian cooking, which are endowed with the flavour of lemon because of the presence of citric oils.*
Tofu *A highly nutritious bean curd, made from soya beans, which is high in protein, low in fat and bland in flavour, which means it takes on other flavours easily.*
Szechuan pepper *Red berries, also known as Chinese pepper, Japanese pepper and anise pepper, with a hot spicy flavour. A peppery addition to soups and sauces.*

Boston Mushroom Soup
AMERICA

There are countless recipes all over the world for mushroom soup. Their success relies, to some degree, on the quality of the mushrooms, and field mushrooms have more flavour than cultivated ones. The tabasco sauce in this recipe adds bite, and dry sherry is always worth adding to virtually any soup.

450 g (1 lb) field mushrooms, sliced
50 g (2 oz) butter
sea salt and freshly ground black pepper
25 g (1 oz) plain flour
600 ml (1 pint) milk
600 ml (1 pint) water
1 teaspoon tabasco sauce
85 ml (3 fl oz) dry sherry
150 ml (¼ pint) single cream
1 tablespoon chopped parsley to garnish

Fry the mushrooms gently in the butter until soft, then season with salt and pepper. Add the flour to make a roux, and cook for 1–2 minutes.

Now add the milk, water, tabasco and sherry, and simmer for 10 minutes. Finally, add the single cream and garnish with parsley.

Serves 4 to 6

Vegetable Soup with Chocolate
MEXICO

The use of chocolate in savoury dishes stems from Mexico and the new world, the most famous Mexican dish being turkey in chilli and chocolate sauce. When chocolate came to Europe, they first drank it as a spiced drink. In Italy they even flavoured pasta with it and in Venice you can still buy tagliatelle which is brown from added cocoa. You need very little chocolate in these savoury dishes.

3 tablespoons olive oil
2 green peppers, cored, seeded and chopped
2 onions, sliced
5 cloves garlic, crushed
2 dried red chillies
1 teaspoon fennel seeds
1 cinnamon stick
1.5 litres (2½ pints) water
3 tablespoons tomato paste
2 tablespoons chopped almonds
50 g (2 oz) bitter chocolate
sea salt and freshly ground black pepper
1 small ripe avocado, peeled and diced

Heat the oil and sauté the peppers, onions and garlic for a few minutes. Grind up the chillies and fennel seeds, and add these, along with the cinnamon stick and water. Simmer for 30 minutes.

Now remove the cinnamon and add the tomato paste, almonds and chocolate. Blend in the liquidiser and season with salt and pepper. Reheat gently. Garnish with diced avocado.

Serves 4 to 6

SALADS, COLD AND WARM

'To make a good salad is to be a brilliant diplomatist —
the problem is entirely the same in both cases.
To know how much oil one must mix with one's vinegar.' Oscar Wilde, 1880

'Salad refreshes without weakening and comforts without irritating.'
Jean-Anthelme Brillat-Savarin, La Physiologie du goût, 1825

'Good cooking does not depend on whether the dish is
large or small, expensive or economical. If one has the art,
then a piece of celery or salted cabbage can be made
into a marvellous delicacy; whereas if one has not the art,
not all the greatest delicacies and rarities of land, sea
or sky are of any avail.' Yuan Mei, Poems trans. Arthur Waley 1956

As with soups, there could easily be a world book of salads, each one a classic. Here are a few which I hope will tempt the reader. Among them are some familiar names, as in the French potato salad and Russian salad, but these recipes, I think, will convince the cook that familiarity should never breed contempt.

We are fortunate now in having many more interesting leaves to choose from and no longer being stuck, in winter, with that tired old hot house lettuce, which has the texture of leather and the colour of a chemical dye. We now have an abundant choice of leaves, wild and cultivated, including lamb's lettuce, rocket, tiny lettuce seedlings, oak leafed lettuce, endive, pak choi, batavia, escarole and Chinese mustard greens.

There is a whole world of salads. There are some where the vegetables are just briefly cooked and then tossed in the dressing and brought to the table warm. There are also cunning mixtures of fruit and vegetables, such as the Turkish Portakal Salatasi and the Philippine Sawsawang Kamatis, which refresh the palate. You can make salads out of almost any ingredient. The essential element is to have a variety of dressings, so ensure that your larder is always well stocked up with different oils and vinegars.

Salade de Roquette aux Capucines
FRANCE

Rocket and nasturtium salad

I could not bear to leave this salad out—another French classic. Even the name is delightful, for the nasturtium flower obviously reminded someone of the head-dress of a Capucine nun. It is also probably the prettiest salad in the world. Nasturtium flowers have a similar flavour to the leaves but are less peppery. Rocket is traditionally considered to be an aphrodisiac and was once banned by the authorities from monastery gardens as it was thought to excite the monks.

generous handful of rocket leaves
generous handful of nasturtium leaves
10–12 nasturtium flowers
Dressing:
2 tablespoons walnut oil
juice and zest of 1 lime
sea salt and freshly ground black pepper

Arrange the rocket and nasturtium leaves in a large salad bowl and place the nasturtium flowers prettily on top.

Mix together all the ingredients for the dressing, but do not dress the salad until just before serving it.

Serves 4 to 6

Salade de Pommes de Terre
FRANCE

Potato salad

This is one of the great French classic recipes but, as with all classics, there are many variations. This is the recipe that I have used many times and which gives me and my family the most pleasure. For the best salad, you will need yellow waxy potatoes: the best varieties are Aura, Bintje, Kipfler, Etoile du Nord, Red Star, Eigenheimer and Pink Fir Apple, all of which can be grown in our gardens.

1 kg (2 lb) new potatoes
1 bunch spring onions, chopped
generous bunch of parsley, finely chopped
300 ml (½ pint) aoili mayonnaise
sprigs of parsley to garnish
Dressing:
85 ml (3 fl oz) olive oil
juice and zest of 1 lemon
3 cloves garlic, crushed
sea salt and freshly ground black pepper

Boil the potatoes in their skins in plenty of lightly salted water. In a large bowl, mix the olive oil with the lemon juice and zest, crushed garlic, and a little sea salt and black pepper.

Drain the potatoes when they are just tender and slice them in 5 mm (¼ inch) pieces, keeping their skins on. Throw the potatoes into a large bowl, dress while they are still warm, and toss vigorously. Add the spring onions and chopped parsley, and then fold in the mayonnaise. Garnish the salad with sprigs of parsley.

Serves 4 to 6

Ensalada de Zanahoria al Jerez
SPAIN
Grated carrots with sherry

This is a marvellously refreshing salad. The raw, grated carrot fused with sherry and a good mustard is absolutely delicious. The red pepper in this recipe is not grilled and skinned as in so many Spanish recipes, and this adds a welcome bitterness to the sweetness of the carrots.

450 g (1 lb) baby carrots, unpeeled
1 red pepper, cored, seeded and diced
1 bunch watercress
Dressing:
3 tablespoons olive oil
1 tablespoon sherry wine vinegar
1 tablespoon dry sherry
1 tablespoon moutarde de Meaux
sea salt and freshly ground black pepper

Grate the carrots into a salad bowl and add the diced red pepper. Trim the stems from the watercress and add the leaves.

Make the dressing by beating together all the ingredients. Immediately before serving, toss the salad in the dressing.

Serves 4 to 6

Radice di Sedano
ITALY
Celeriac with mustard sauce

While we in Britain are just discovering celeriac, the rest of Europe has been enjoying it for centuries. This salad is not unlike the French rémoulade, but is slightly richer and more highly flavoured. It makes a superb first course.

2 medium celeriacs
zest and juice of 1 lemon
1 teaspoon sea salt
1 bunch spring onions, thinly sliced
generous handful of parsley, finely chopped
Dressing:
1 tablespoon Dijon mustard
sea salt and freshly ground black pepper
85 ml (3 fl oz) soured cream or mayonnaise

Peel the celeriac then grate into a bowl. Add the lemon zest and juice, and the salt, and cover with water. Leave for 1 hour, then drain and dry completely, squeezing out the moisture with your hands.

Place in a salad bowl and add the spring onions and parsley. Finally, beat the mustard and seasonings into the soured cream or mayonnaise, pour the dressing over the salad, and toss.

Serves 4 to 6

Fasolia Mavromitika
GREECE
Black-eyed bean salad

Greece abounds in many kinds of bean salad, which can be eaten warm or cold. This one, with its black-eyed beans, looks particularly pretty. Make sure they do not overcook and break up.

225 g (8 oz) black-eyed beans
2 onions, finely sliced
generous bunch of parsley, finely choppped
5 tablespoons olive oil
1 tablespoon oregano
1 tablespoon wine vinegar
sea salt and freshly ground black pepper

Pour boiling water over the beans and soak them for 1 hour. Then bring them to the boil and simmer for 30 minutes, until they are just tender. Drain.

Return the beans to the pan and quickly add all the other ingredients so that the onions soften a little in the heat of the beans. Place a lid on the pan and give it a good shake. Eat the salad warm.

Serves 4 to 6

Black-eyed beans *Also known as cow peas, these are cream-coloured and kidney shaped, and have a distinctive black spot or 'eye'—hence their name. They probably originated in Africa but are now grown in many tropical countries, especially in the southern USA.*

Salata ot Suror Spanak
RUMANIA
Spinach and yoghurt salad

Spinach and yoghurt go together particularly well. This salad appears in many different forms all over the Balkan countries.

2 large onions, thinly sliced
150 ml (¼ pint) wine vinegar
225 g (8 oz) young, fresh spinach
150 ml (¼ pint) natural yoghurt
2 tablespoons olive oil
1 tablespoon green peppercorns
sea salt and freshly ground black pepper

The day before, place the sliced onions in a bowl with the vinegar. Marinate for 12 hours.

Wash and dry the spinach leaves, discard the stalks, tear neatly into small pieces and place in a salad bowl. Drain the onion and add to the spinach, reserving the vinegar for use as a dressing for another dish. Mix together everything else, pour over the salad and toss thoroughly.

Serves 4 to 6

Russian Salad
RUSSIA

This salad, sadly, has become synonymous with canning and, what is now almost an anachronism, the hors d'oeuvres trolley in grand hotels. If you bother to make it yourself, however, it is one of the most delicious salads in the world and deserves to be a classic. It is, of course, best eaten in the summer and goes beautifully with a wide range of different salads as a light supper.

225 g (8 oz) cooked new potatoes, diced
120 g (4 oz) cooked French beans, sliced
3 cooked baby carrots, sliced
50 g (2 oz) cooked haricot beans
1½ tablespoons olive oil
½ tablespoon white wine vinegar
sea salt and freshly ground black pepper
1 hard-boiled egg
1 tablespoon capers
1 tablespoon gherkins, chopped
1 tablespoon finely chopped parsley
1 tablespoon finely chopped mint
aioli mayonnaise to taste

Mix together all the vegetables in a large bowl with the oil, vinegar, salt and pepper. Chill for 2 hours.

Just before serving, chop the hard-boiled egg and add to the salad with the capers, gherkins and herbs. Finally, fold in the mayonnaise.

Serves 4 to 6

Portakal Salatasi
TURKEY
Orange and onion salad

In the Middle East, they make various salads with fruit, including this one where the main ingredients are oranges and onions. Choose the red onions, which are sweet as opposed to pungent. This is an excellent salad to serve with curries and other spicy dishes.

4 oranges
1 batavia
3 red onions, sliced in rings
2 tablespoons capers
75 g (3 oz) black olives, stoned
Dressing:
1 tablespoon white wine vinegar
1 tablespoon whole seed mustard
4 tablespoons olive oil
sea salt and freshly ground black pepper

Cut away the zest of the oranges and reserve for the dressing. Remove all the orange skin and pith, and slice the oranges in rounds.

Arrange the batavia leaves on a large serving platter, and lay the orange slices on top, then the onion rings, and sprinkle over the capers and black olives. Make the dressing, using all the remaining ingredients and the orange zest. Pour over the salad and serve.

Serves 4 to 6

Koosmali
INDIA
Carrot, mustard and peanut salad

Salads of grated hot vegetables, served warm and tossed in hot spices, are legion in the sub-Continent. This is a great favourite of mine because the sweetness of carrots offsets the hot chillies and yoghurt.

3 tablespoons sunflower oil
2 teaspoons mustard seeds
1 teaspoon asofoetida (see page 33)
2 green chillies, sliced
1 tablespoon sugar
750 g (1½ lb) carrots, grated
1 tablespoon lime juice
3 tablespoons natural yoghurt or soured cream
3 tablespoons roasted peanuts, coarsely chopped
few chopped coriander leaves to garnish

Heat the sunflower oil in a pan and throw in the mustard seeds. When they begin to pop, add the asofoetida, chillies and sugar. Cook for a moment to melt the sugar, then throw in the grated carrots, shake and stir the pan, cooking the carrots for 2–3 minutes. Then pour into a bowl.

When cool, mix the lime juice with the yoghurt or soured cream. Add the chopped peanuts to the salad and toss it in the dressing. Sprinkle a few chopped coriander leaves over the top.

Serves 4 to 6

Hot Sweet Rice Salad
CHINA

This is a delicious warm fruit salad and goes well with a lunch of varied dim sum.

50 g (2 oz) raisins
50 g (2 oz) currants
3 tablespoons light soy sauce
2 tablespoons dry sherry
4 tablespoons sunflower oil
450 g (1 lb) cooked patna rice
1 small cucumber, diced
25 g (1 oz) ginger, grated
120 g (4 oz) seedless grapes
1 tablespoon sugar
sea salt and freshly ground black pepper

Soak the raisins and currants in the soy sauce and sherry, and leave for 1 hour.

Heat the oil in a pan and throw in the rice, cucumber and ginger. Gently fry for a few minutes, until the cucumber becomes crisp, then add all the remaining ingredients. Stir fry until hot, then serve warm.

Serves 4 to 6

Sawsawang Kamatis
PHILIPPINES
Tomato and mango salad

Salads that combine fruits with vegetables can be excellent. This one mixes ripe sweetness with sourness, which is particularly good in the summer.

450 g (1 lb) ripe tomatoes, sliced
1 ripe mango, sliced
1 green, unripe mango, grated
15 g (½ oz) fresh ginger, grated
1 dried red chilli, seeded and flaked
sea salt and freshly ground black pepper

Arrange the tomatoes and ripe mango in alternate lines on a serving platter. Sprinkle the grated unripe mango and ginger over the top.

Then sprinkle the flaked chilli, salt and pepper over that. Leave to cool for 30 minutes.

Serves 4 to 6

Daikon Namasn
JAPAN
Carrot and radish salad

There are many salads using the daikon, or white radish. This one gives the root a kick by using wasabi powder, or Japanese horseradish. Do remember to mix the powder and leave it for 15 minutes before using, as it needs this time to mature.

1 daikon
1 teaspoon sea salt
½ teaspoon wasabi powder
2 tablespoons light soy sauce
2 tablespoons sesame oil
1 tablespoon rice vinegar
2 teaspoons sugar
3–4 baby carrots

Slice the daikon into julienne strips. Salt lightly and allow to stand for 1 hour, then squeeze out the moisture with your hands.

To make the dressing, mix the wasabi powder with all the other ingredients. Allow to stand for 15 minutes, then pour over the daikon and carrots, and toss thoroughly.

Serves 4 to 6

Daikon _Also known as mooli, this is a long white radish, grown in Japan. It is available all year round and can be eaten either raw in salads or cooked in savoury dishes._
Wasabi _This is the green-coloured root of a Japanese plant, with a hot taste similar to that of horseradish or mustard. It is sold in most Japanese stores in powdered form._

Yam Taeng Kwa
THAILAND
Cucumber salad

Amazingly enough, this fiery little salad is wonderfully refreshing on a hot day. I have eaten this salad, and others like it, as a mid-morning snack in the steamy, riotous crowds of Bangkok, and in that climate it has the same effect as drinking a Scotch on a winter's day.

1 cucumber, diced
2 courgettes, grated
1 teaspoon sea salt
1 onion, grated
2 tablespoons sesame oil
zest and juice of 2 limes
2 tablespoons peanuts, roasted and roughly chopped
2 dried red chillies, seeded and broken into flakes
szechuan pepper (see page 36)
1 tablespoon caster sugar
lettuce leaves to garnish

Salt the cucumber and courgettes and leave to stand for 1 hour. Then drain and squeeze out all the moisture.

Place in a mixing bowl with the grated onion. Add all the remaining ingredients except for the lettuce leaves and mix thoroughly. Cover a serving platter with lettuce leaves and pile the salad up on top.

Serves 4 to 6

Caesar Salad
AMERICA

This salad was created during prohibition by Caesar Cardini, the owner of a restaurant in Tijuana, Mexico. Like all great classic dishes, there have been many additions and variations, most of which now include anchovies, bacon or blue cheese, but this is the original recipe. It was eaten with the hands, using lettuce leaves to scoop up the sauce and croûtons. The undercooked egg mixed with oil creates a very light mayonnaise.

2 Cos or romaine lettuces
2 eggs
6 tablespoons olive oil
3 cloves garlic, crushed
sea salt and freshly ground pepper
1 teaspoon Worcestershire sauce
juice and zest of 1 lemon
25 g (1 oz) Parmesan cheese, freshly grated
50 g (2 oz) wholewheat garlic croûtons

Break the lettuce leaves from the central stalk, wash and refrigerate in a plastic bag for 1 hour. Boil the eggs for 1 minute exactly, then plunge into cold water to stop them cooking any longer.

Pour the olive oil into a large salad bowl, add the lettuce and toss well. Add the garlic, salt and pepper, Worcestershire sauce, lemon juice and zest. Then add the peeled eggs, ensuring that you scoop out all the thin layer of cooked white near the shell. Toss again, then sprinkle with grated Parmesan cheese and croûtons.

Serves 4 to 6

Ensalada Mixta
MEXICO
Mixed vegetable salad

On the face of it, this looks not unlike Russian Salad, but the use of fresh coriander leaves, feta cheese and lime juice gives it its own strong particular flavours.

225 g (8 oz) baby carrots
225 g (8 oz) potatoes
225 g (8 oz) French beans
225 g (8 oz) peas
1 large Cos lettuce
450 g (1 lb) tomatoes, sliced
1 large onion, sliced
1 cucumber, sliced
1 bunch radishes
1 bunch watercress
1 hard-boiled egg
3 tablespoons crumbled feta cheese (see page 14)
1 bunch of coriander leaves, chopped
5 tablespoons olive oil
zest and juice of 2 limes
sea salt and freshly ground black pepper

Cook the vegetables until tender, then dice the carrots and potatoes and slice the beans.

Arrange the Cos lettuce leaves in a large salad bowl. Put the cooked vegetables with the tomatoes, onion and cucumber into another bowl. Add the whole radishes. Discard the stems of the watercress and add the leaves. Mash the egg with the crumbled feta cheese, then add the chopped coriander leaves. Finally, add the olive oil, lime zest and juice, salt and pepper. Pour over the chopped vegetables, toss well and pile on top of the lettuce leaves.

Serves 10

<u>BREAD</u>

'When God gives hard bread He gives sharp teeth.' **German Proverb**

*'More eating of corn bread would I'm sure make a better foundation
for an American literature. The white bread we eat
is to corn bread what Hollywood will be to real American dramatic
literature when it comes.'* **Sherwood Anderson, Memoirs**

Bread is, of course, one of man's earliest foods. It goes back some 10,000 years. The first bread would have been unleavened, a kind of dried porridge, highly grained, a little like a thick ship's biscuit. But there is also a theory that if the mix for the dough was left even for a short period of time, it would have been attacked by the wild yeasts in the air, which would soon have leavened the bread; the idea that early civilisation had unleavened bread is therefore probably an erroneous one. There are other starters than yeast—almost anything, in fact, including sour milk, flour, water and potato.

Grass seed (the first wheat) was first cultivated in Mesopotamia in 8000BC and then, some 3,000 years later, it was grown in Egypt along the banks of the Nile. It was not long before grain and breads became staple foods and spread north to Greece and the Balkans. It was in around 3200BC that we have the first recorded evidence of the cultivation of grain in Britain.

It is climate which dictates exactly how bread is made. In hot countries, bread can be baked on a flat stone or iron plate. In northern countries, it is baked in enclosed brick ovens, making leavened bread. So the flat bread belongs to the Middle and Far East, Africa and South America. For the most part, however, the breads tend to be not so very different, though the grain used imparts a distinctive flavour, but there is actually little else to distinguish a chapati from a tortilla, for example, so I have not included many unleavened breads so as to allow more room for others.

Crumpets
SCOTLAND

We are all familiar with commercial crumpets, but these home-made ones are quite different as they are not so spongy and have more flavour. You can, of course, have added flavour if you make them with wholemeal flour, or even half wholemeal and half plain. No one seems to know how far back crumpets go, though they are obviously related to the technique of drop scones and would originally surely have been eaten around the fire as soon as they were cooked.

1 tablespoon caster sugar
1 egg, beaten
½ teaspoon cream of tartar
½ teaspoon bicarbonate of soda
120 g (4 oz) plain flour, sifted
150 ml (1 pint) milk
pinch of salt

Beat the sugar and egg to a cream. Add the raising agents to the flour, then add this mixture to the egg and sugar, and finally add the milk and salt. Stir thoroughly.

Using a heavy-bottomed dry pan or griddle, drop spoonfuls of the mixture into the pan and cook for 2½–3 minutes until the bottom is set. Then turn them over to brown on the other side. Allow to cool and serve.

Makes 10

Bara Brith
WALES

This is an old Welsh recipe for fruit bread which is made extra delicious by the inclusion of candied peel. If you prefer, you can make the dough darker and richer by adding one-third rye flour instead of using all wholemeal.

75 g (3 oz) currants
75 g (3 oz) raisins
300 ml (½ pint) milk
25 g (1 oz) candied peel, chopped
50 g (2 oz) soft brown sugar
75 g (3 oz) butter
450 g (1 lb) wholemeal flour, sifted
1 sachet active dried yeast
1 teaspoon salt
1 teaspoon mixed spice

Soak the dried fruit in the milk overnight. Drain and reserve the milk. Mix the dried fruit, candied peel and sugar together, and place in a warm oven for a few minutes. Heat the butter with the reserved milk until the butter has melted. Leave to cool until just lukewarm.

Mix all the dry ingredients together, then add the milk. Knead for 5 minutes. Butter a 450 g (1 lb) loaf pan and place the dough in it. Cover and leave to rise for 1 hour.

Bake the loaf in a preheated oven, at 200°C (400°F), Gas Mark 6, for 30 minutes, protecting the top with buttered paper for the last 10 minutes.

Makes 450 g (1 lb) loaf

Soda Bread
IRELAND

This is one of the most familiar of all unleavened breads. The raising agent here is the buttermilk, as well as bicarbonate of soda. These breads are delicious eaten straight from the oven.

225 g (8 oz) wholemeal flour, sifted
225 g (8 oz) strong white bread flour, sifted
1½ teaspoons bicarbonate of soda
2 teaspoons salt
300 ml (½ pint) sour buttermilk
2 tablespoons warm water (optional)

Mix the flours, bicarbonate of soda and salt together thoroughly. Add the buttermilk and mix to a dough. If it is too dry, add the warm water. Divide into two and flatten each quantity of dough into a large scone shape. Using a sharp knife, score a cross on top so that the loaf will divide easily into four.

Place on a baking tray and cover with a cake tin. Bake in a preheated oven, at 220°C (425°F), Gas Mark 7, for 30 minutes. Take the cake tin off the loaf and bake for a further 10 minutes.

Makes 450 g (1 lb) loaf

Waffles
HOLLAND

Waffles are highly addictive. The only way of not becoming addicted to these is never to buy a waffle iron. If you have a family, however, you'll find that young children adore them and you can eat them with virtually any kind of topping, sweet or savoury.

120 g (4 oz) plain flour, sifted
15 g (½ oz) bicarbonate of soda
15 g (½ oz) cream of tartar
¼ teaspoon salt
½ teaspoon sugar
1 egg, beaten
50 g (2 oz) butter, melted
150 ml (¼ pint) buttermilk

Mix together the flour, raising agents, salt and sugar. Add the egg and melted butter to the buttermilk and pour into the flour mixture. Mix to a batter.

Lightly oil the insides of a waffle iron and fill the bottom half with batter. Follow the manufacturer's instructions for cooking. Serve hot with butter.

Makes 6 to 8

Zopf
SWITZERLAND

This is the famous plaited loaf which is traditionally eaten in Switzerland with Sunday dinner. It is not at all difficult to make.

450 g (1 lb) strong white bread flour, sifted
8 g (¼ oz) dried yeast
50 g (2 oz) butter
250 ml (8 fl oz) tepid milk
½ teaspoon salt
1 egg, beaten
1 egg yolk diluted with 1 tablespoon water to glaze

Mix together the flour and yeast. Melt the butter in the milk, add the salt and egg, and mix everything together thoroughly. Knead for 5 minutes. Cover and leave to rise for 1 hour.

Divide into three. Roll each piece into a long sausage shape. Plait from the centre down towards you, then turn it over and plait the other half. Cover and leave to rise for another 30 minutes.

Glaze with diluted egg yolk, then place on a baking tray and bake in a preheated oven, at 200°C (400°F), Gas Mark 6, for 40 minutes.

Makes 450 g (1 lb) loaf

Pain aux Noix
FRANCE
Walnut bread

This is one of the great classic bread recipes and is not in the least difficult to make. The marvellous aroma of walnuts as it bakes will make the salivary glands work overtime.

225 g (8 oz) wholemeal flour, sifted
225 g (8 oz) strong white bread flour, sifted
15 g (½ oz) dried yeast
2 tablespoons walnut oil
2 tablespoons honey
300 ml (½ pint) tepid water
½ teaspoon salt
175 g (6 oz) walnuts, roughly crushed
beaten egg to glaze

Mix together all the ingredients, except for the walnuts and the egg for glazing. Knead for 5 minutes and leave to prove for 1 hour. Knock down the dough, roll out, scatter the walnuts on top, then fold up the dough and leave to prove for 20 minutes.

Place on a baking tray, slash the loaf with a cross and glaze the top. Bake in a preheated oven, at 220°C (425°F), Gas Mark 7, for 40 minutes or until the loaf sounds hollow when tapped.

Makes 450 g (1 lb) loaf

Pumpernickel
GERMANY
Black bread

A bread made from rye flour is still highly popular in Scandinavia and in both central and eastern Europe. This particular bread is delicious with cheese.

750 g (1½ lb) rye flour, sifted
25 g (1 oz) dried yeast
50 g (2 oz) butter
5 tablespoons molasses
150 ml (¼ pint) warm water
1 teaspoon salt
1 egg, beaten
2 tablespoons caraway seeds
1 egg yolk diluted with 1 tablespoon water to glaze

Mix the flour and yeast together. Add the butter and molasses to the warm water and melt both, then pour into the flour when still warm, adding the salt and the beaten egg. Mix thoroughly, then knead for 5 minutes.

Divide the mixture into two and place in two well-greased 450 g (1 lb) bread tins. Cover and leave to prove. Bake in a preheated oven, at 200°C (400°F), Gas Mark 6, for 30 minutes. Glaze the top with the diluted egg yolk, sprinkle with caraway seeds and bake for a further 10 minutes. Leave to cool and slice thinly.

Makes two 450 g (1 lb) loaves

Pizza
ITALY

Your own home-made pizza tastes far better than any you can buy except, perhaps, the ones made in Naples. You can, of course, make your pizza with half wholemeal flour to give the crust greater flavour.

Dough:
225 g (8 oz) strong white flour, sifted
½ teaspoon salt
15 g (½ oz) fresh yeast
2 tablespoons warmed milk
1 egg, beaten
2 tablespoons olive oil
2–3 tablespoons warm water
Filling:
2 tablespoons olive oil
2 onions, sliced
1 green pepper, cored, seeded and sliced
5 cloves garlic, crushed
1 teaspoon oregano
1 x 400 g (14 oz) can tomatoes
2 tablespoons tomato purée
sea salt and freshly ground black pepper
5 fresh tomatoes, sliced
12 black olives, stoned
2 tablespoons capers

Mix together the flour and salt in a large mixing bowl. Place the yeast in a cup and pour the warmed milk over it. Stir and leave to ferment for about 10 minutes. Once it has fermented, add the creamed yeast to the flour and then add the beaten egg, olive oil and warm water. Stir well.

Start to work the dough with your hands. Knead it until it becomes smooth and elastic. Form the dough into a ball and leave in a covered bowl in a warm place for 2 hours to allow it to rise.

While the dough is rising, make the filling. Heat the olive oil in a pan and add the onions, pepper, garlic and oregano. Fry gently for about 10 minutes, then add the canned tomatoes. Simmer the mixture for 45 minutes, by which time you should have a thick, rich sauce. Add the tomato purée, salt and pepper, and cook for another 5 minutes.

Oil a 30 x 45 cm (12 x 14 inch) baking sheet. Take the ball of risen dough and smooth it down over the baking sheet, pressing and pulling it out. Make a small ridge of dough around the edge of the baking sheet. Leave to rest for 10 minutes.

Smear the filling over the dough and garnish with slices of fresh tomato, black olives and capers. Rest the pizza again for another 10 minutes. Bake in a preheated oven, at 220°C (425°F), Gas Mark 7, for 15 minutes. Then turn the oven down to 180°C (350°F), Gas Mark 4 and bake for a further 15 minutes.

Serves 4 to 6

Toutmanik
BULGARIA
Layered cheese bread

This is a superb rich loaf which is perfect for a dinner party.

175 g (6 oz) strong white bread flour, sifted
50 g (2 oz) wholemeal flour, sifted
15 g (½ oz) dried yeast
½ teaspoon sea salt
150 ml (¼ pint) tepid water
120 g (4 oz) butter, melted
225 g (8 oz) feta cheese (see page 14)
2 eggs, beaten
1 tablespoon oregano
freshly ground black pepper

Thoroughly mix together the flours, yeast, salt and water to make a dough. Knead for 5 minutes, cover and leave for 1 hour to prove. Knock back the dough, roll into a long sausage and slice into eight.

Flour a board and roll each piece into a circle to fit a round cake or bread tin. Make two piles of four each, painting the top of each one with a little melted butter, leaving the top of each pile unpainted.

Crumble the feta in a bowl and add most of the beaten egg, the oregano and the rest of the melted butter. Season with black pepper. Place the first pile in the buttered cake tin, pour over the cheese mixture, and place the second pile on top. Prick with a fork and leave to prove for 1 hour.

Bake on the top shelf of a preheated oven, at 180°C (350°F), Gas Mark 4, for 45 minutes. After 30 minutes, glaze the top with the reserved beaten egg.

Makes a large loaf

Bagels
RUMANIA

Bagels are eaten all over western Europe but this is quite the best way to cook them.

350 g (12 oz) white flour, sifted
25 g (1 oz) dried yeast
3 tablespoons honey
4 tablespoons corn oil
1 egg, beaten
150 ml (¼ pint) tepid water
1 egg yolk, diluted with 1 tablespoon cold water to glaze
poppy seeds to decorate

Mix together the flour and yeast and add 1 tablespoon of honey, the oil, egg and water. Knead for 5 minutes. Leave to prove for 1 hour.

Divide the dough into 12 pieces. Roll each one into a thin sausage, then pinch the ends together, so that they make small circles. Leave to rest, covered, for 15 minutes.

Fill a large saucepan with water, bring to the boil and add the rest of the honey. Drop the bagels in the simmering water and poach gently for 15 minutes. They are done when they rise to the surface.

Take them out with a slotted spoon and drain well. Lay on a baking sheet and glaze with the diluted egg yolk, then sprinkle with poppy seeds. Bake in a preheated oven, at 200°C (400°F), Gas Mark 6, for 30 minutes, or until crisp and brown.

Makes 12

Black Olive Bread
CRETE

The smell of oregano, garlic and olives seems to permeate the islands of Greece. All three ingredients come together in this marvellous rich peasant bread, which is so good to eat especially with feta cheese.

450 g (1 lb) strong white bread flour, sifted
120 g (4 oz) wholemeal flour, sifted
1 teaspoon sea salt
25 g (1 oz) dried yeast
2 tablespoons olive oil
350 ml (12 fl oz) tepid water
6 cloves garlic, finely chopped
1 onion, finely chopped
12 black olives, stoned and finely chopped
1 tablespoon finely chopped oregano
1 tablespoon finely chopped mint

Mix together the two flours, salt, yeast, olive oil and water. Knead for 5 minutes, then leave to prove for 1 hour.

Mix together the garlic, onion, olives and herbs. Punch down the dough, roll it out, and scatter the filling over it. Fold up the dough into a ball and leave to rise for another 1 hour.

Place the dough on a baking sheet. Bake in a preheated oven, at 220°C (425°F), Gas Mark 7, for 45 minutes.

Makes a large loaf

Falofel *A popular Israeli snack, these are little balls of chick peas ground up with herbs and spices.*

Khubz
EGYPT
Pitta bread

Pitta bread is really street food. All over the Middle East, these breads are split and filled with various stuffings, falofels, pickles or salads.

450 g (1 lb) strong white bread flour, sifted
25 g (1 oz) dried yeast
300 ml (½ pint) warm water
2 tablespoons olive oil
pinch of salt

Mix all the ingredients together and knead for 10 minutes. Leave for 1 hour to rise. Divide the dough into eight balls, flour each one and roll out to a circle.

Leave them to rise again, then slip on to a baking sheet and bake in a preheated oven, at 220°C (425°F), Gas Mark 7, for 20 minutes. They can be reheated under the grill, when they will brown a little further.

Makes 8

Stuffed Tandoor Bread
INDIA

This recipe for stuffed tandoor bread is obviously influenced by the Middle Eastern pitta bread.

Stuffing:
120 g (4 oz) ricotta or paneer cheese
3 green chillies, seeded and finely chopped
handful of coriander, finely chopped
2 teaspoons lemon juice
sea salt and freshly ground black pepper
Bread:
50 g (2 oz) butter
65 ml (2½ fl oz) milk
25 g (1 oz) dried yeast
½ teaspoon sugar
½ teaspoon salt
175 g (6 oz) self-raising flour, sifted

First make the stuffing. Combine all the ingredients and mix well.

To make the bread, melt the butter into the milk. Mix the yeast, sugar and salt with the flour. Add the liquid. Knead for 5 minutes, cover and let the dough rise for 1 hour. Knock down the dough and knead again for a moment.

Divide into four portions and roll each portion into a ball. Make a dent in the balls and place a spoonful of the stuffing in each, roll the ball again in your hands so that the stuffing is in the centre. Then, using a rolling pin, roll carefully into a circle. Place the rolled, stuffed dough on a baking sheet and bake in a preheated oven, at 190°C (375°F), Gas Mark 5, for 5 minutes. Place under a hot grill before serving so that they are flecked brown.

Makes 4

Chapati
INDIA

This recipe from India is an unleavened bread and should always be eaten as soon as it is cooked.

50 g (2 oz) wholemeal flour, sifted
50 g (2 oz) strong white bread flour, sifted
1 teaspoon corn oil
pinch of salt
85 ml (3 fl oz) warm water

Mix the flours together with the oil and salt, then add half of the water and continue to mix so that all the flour is moistened. Gradually add the rest of the water until the dough begins to form, then knead it for 5 minutes. This is best done with dough hooks in a food processor.

When the dough is soft and pliable, leave it to prove, covered, for 1 hour. Then form into eight small balls. Dust these with flour and roll them out into eight circles. Cook them for about 30 seconds on each side on a griddle or hot plate. Have ready a rack standing over a flame and lay the chapatis on this for only about 15 seconds, or until the chapatis have browned in spots and puffed up a little. Serve as soon as they are cooked.

Makes 8

Ricotta *is a soft, mild Italian cheese made from the whey of cow's milk.* **Paneer cheese** *is an Indian version of this.*

Muffins
AMERICA

Recipes for muffins are one of the most popular in the States. The Americans add a great variety of things to this basic recipe, including blueberries, dried fruit, butter and jam or, for a savoury muffin, cheese and sweetcorn.

225 g (8 oz) plain flour, sifted
1 teaspoon bicarbonate of soda
1 teaspoon cream of tartar
½ teaspoon salt
25 g (1 oz) sugar
1 egg, beaten
50 g (2 oz) butter, melted
300 ml (½ pint) milk

Mix together the flour, raising agents, salt and sugar. Then mix together the beaten egg, melted butter and milk and add this to the dry ingredients. Mix into a batter.

Grease a bun tin and half fill the cups. Bake in a preheated oven, at 200°C (400°F), Gas Mark 6, for 20 minutes or until risen and brown.

Makes 8 to 10

Tortillas
MEXICO
Corn bread

This is the bread of Mexico which is dipped into stews and soups or wrapped around various fillings. The maize flour gives it a wonderful dark flavour, which I believe goes particularly well with the chillies and beans with which it is associated.

120 g (4 oz) maza harina, sifted
120 g (4 oz) wholemeal flour, sifted
1 teaspoon sea salt
250 ml (8 fl oz) water

It is best to make this in a food processor with dough hooks. Mix the flours and salt together and gradually add the water, kneading all the time, until you have a firm dough.

Roll out the dough into a long sausage shape and cut into 12 pieces. Roll each one into a ball and then roll into a 15 cm (6 inch) circle between sheets of greaseproof paper. Cook each tortilla for about 1 minute on each side in a dry, heavy frying pan. Remove and cover with greaseproof paper.

Makes 12

Maza harina *A coarse flour made from corn cobs, otherwise known as corn meal or maize meal. The Italians use a coarser version of this to make their famous polenta.*

EGG DISHES

*'To Aunt Irene the Ten Commandments seemed
almost insignificant compared with
the astonishing miracle of what you could do with an egg.
As the angel had left in his fiery chariot
he must have asked, "And don't forget omelettes and cakes
and custard and soufflés and poaching and frying and
boiling and baking." '.* The 27th Kingdom, *Alice Thomas Ellis*

It is climate which dictates how common egg dishes
are. Because eggs marry so often with dairy
produce, you do not find many egg recipes in hot
countries. There is generally no pasture for dairy
herds, though in the hottest climates you will, of
course, find egg-laying hens. There, the eggs are
cooked at once and eaten hard boiled. To keep them
would be impossible without a refrigerator. So
there is no time for an egg cuisine to evolve.

Egg cuisine is more sophisticated, perhaps, in
western Europe, than anywhere else. Compare the
soufflé with the Middle Eastern Eggah, and the
difference between haute cuisine and hearty peasant
cooking is obvious.

The egg dishes included here tend to be simple —
for these are generally the best. They are flavoured
with whatever is the most characteristic spice or
vegetable of each country. So in Russia it is
horseradish, in Italy tomato, in Japan tofu, and in
India spices and chillies.

Chutneyed Eggs
IRELAND

This is an idea from Myrtle Allen's Ballymaloe house, where they have a cold buffet on Sunday nights. It is very simple, but unexpectedly good. It can be served as part of a first course, or as an appetiser at a party.

6 free-range eggs
50 g (2 oz) butter, softened
1 tablespoon strong chutney
sea salt and freshly ground black pepper
parsley or gherkins to garnish

Hard boil the eggs, peel and slice them in half. Take out the yolks and mix them thoroughly with all the other ingredients. Pile back into the egg whites and garnish with a little parsley or sliced gherkin.

Makes 12

Piperade
FRANCE

I am particularly fond of this dish as it was one of the very first French dishes I ever cooked for myself, following an early Elizabeth David recipe, and I was thunderstruck at how delicious it was. It still remains a favourite today and I often make it in the summer months as either a light supper or a first course.

50 ml (2 fl oz) olive oil
1 green pepper, seeded and sliced
1 red pepper, seeded and sliced
1 yellow pepper, seeded and sliced
1 large onion, finely sliced
450 g (1 lb) tomatoes, peeled and chopped
6 eggs, beaten
sea salt and freshly ground black pepper

Heat the olive oil in a shallow pan and throw in the peppers and onion. Cook over a low heat for about 10 minutes until they become soft. Add the tomatoes and cook for another 10 minutes or so, until all the vegetables have made a thick sauce. Pour in the eggs, season with salt and pepper, and beat with a fork until all the ingredients amalgamate and the eggs set the mixture.

Serves 4 to 6

Uova Affogate in Sugo di Pomodoro
ITALY
Eggs poached in tomato sauce

This is another favourite recipe of mine. So often a poached egg is ruined by being too watery or tasting of the vinegar that has been added to the poaching water, but here the eggs are poached in the tomato sauce and soak up that unforgettable flavour of ripe, sweet tomatoes with basil.

750 g (1½ lb) ripe tomatoes
2 cloves garlic, crushed
handful of basil, chopped
sea salt and freshly ground black pepper
6 free-range eggs

First make the sauce. Chop the tomatoes roughly, throw them into a saucepan with the garlic, basil and seasonings. Place over low heat, put the lid on the saucepan and allow the tomatoes to simmer in their own juice for 10 minutes. Leave to cool, then pour through a sieve into a shallow pan, discarding the skin and pips.

Heat the sauce so that it is bubbly and make a hollow with the back of the spoon as you slip an egg into it. Cook the eggs gently until the whites are set. Eat with good wholemeal toast or mop up the sauce with crusty fresh bread.

Serves 4 to 6

Mojete
SPAIN
Egg and potato casserole

This is an interesting recipe from Spain which has much of the charm of a one-pot meal and makes an excellent supper or luncheon dish. The eggs are steamed over the vegetables in the last few minutes. Make sure the egg yolks do not harden, so that they can be mixed with the potato.

85 ml (3 fl oz) olive oil
5 cloves garlic, crushed
1 teaspoon hot pimento powder
2 bay leaves
1 sprig rosemary
1 kg (2 lb) potatoes, peeled, sliced and salted
4–6 eggs

Use a thick-bottomed casserole. Pour in the olive oil and throw in the garlic, pimento powder, bay leaves and rosemary. Add the sliced potatoes, cover and cook over a low heat for 30 minutes or until the potatoes are tender. Break the eggs in on top of the potatoes and let them steam for 5 minutes or until the whites are set.

Serves 4 to 6

Open Filo Egg and Yoghurt Pie
BULGARIA

It is the Middle East which has made filo pastry famous, and it was the Turks who took it to eastern Europe and to the walls of Vienna. This is, traditionally, a Lenten pie but so delicious that it would be absolutely no punishment to eat.

8 sheets of filo pastry (see page 15)
6 eggs
300 ml (½ pint) yoghurt
120 g (4 oz) feta cheese, crumbled (see page 14)
freshly ground black pepper
50 g (2 oz) breadcrumbs

Butter a shallow pie dish and lay the filo pastry in it, buttering the layers as you go. Trim the outside. Beat the eggs, yoghurt, cheese and pepper thoroughly together. Pour into the pie dish and sprinkle with breadcrumbs. Bake in a preheated oven, at 190°C (375°F), Gas Mark 5, for 30 minutes, or until risen and light brown. Leave to rest for a few minutes before slicing.

Serves 4 to 6

Menensen
TURKEY
Tomato, cheese and pepper omelette

This omelette looks very pretty when it is served, for it is flecked with the green of the pepper and the red of the tomato. It is sometimes scrambled and used as a filling in pitta bread.

3 tablespoons olive oil
2 green peppers, seeded and sliced
3 cloves garlic, crushed
450 g (1 lb) tomatoes, peeled and chopped
1 teaspoon oregano
120 g (4 oz) feta cheese, crumbled or diced (see page 14)
sea salt and freshly ground black pepper
6 eggs, beaten

Heat the oil in a pan and throw in the peppers and garlic. Fry gently for 5 minutes, then add the tomatoes and oregano. Simmer for 10 minutes, then add the feta cheese and seasonings.

Cook for another minute or until the cheese begins to melt, then pour in the eggs. Mix lightly until the eggs have set the mixture, rather like a piperade.

Serves 4 to 6

Pechoniye Yaitza
RUSSIA
Grilled stuffed eggs

These make a very good first course. I particularly like the fact that the eggs are served in their shells. The flavouring is, of course, characteristically Russian. I have made this dish with duck eggs and the blue colour of the shell adds much at the table.

6 large, hard-boiled eggs
1 tablespoon horseradish
2 tablespoons butter
generous handful of chopped dill
1 teaspoon paprika
pinch of sea salt

Using a very sharp knife, slice the eggs in half in their shells. Carefully remove the eggs and place in a bowl with all the other ingredients, then mash with a fork or place in a food processor or liquidiser and mix thoroughly. Return the egg mixture to the shells and place under a hot grill until the tops are brown and buttery.

Makes 12

Dill *A member of the parsley family, dill is used for both its seeds, which are slightly bitter, and its leaves, which can be fresh or dried and have a mild flavour reminiscent of caraway and are used in pickles, egg and vegetables dishes, soups, sauces and salads. Dill weed refers to the fresh green leaves.*

Eggah
EGYPT
Thick vegetable omelette

This kind of omelette appears all over the Middle East. It is often taken on picnics and eaten cold.

4 tablespoons olive oil
50 g (2 oz) courgettes, diced
50 g (2 oz) potatoes
50 g (2 oz) onions, chopped
50 g (2 oz) leeks, chopped
50 g (2 oz) mushrooms, sliced
50 g (2 oz) dried spinach, finely shredded
4 cloves garlic, crushed
sea salt and freshly ground black pepper
generous handful of chopped parsley
6 eggs, beaten

Heat the olive oil in a shallow heavy-bottomed pan and throw in all the vegetables, garlic and seasonings. Cook slowly over a gentle flame for about 20 minutes, or until the potatoes are tender.

Mix the parsley and the eggs together, pour over the vegetables and let the eggs set at the base. Place under a hot grill to cook the top.

Serves 10

Kooku
IRAN
Potato omelette

This omelette is not so very far removed from the Egyptian Eggah, and a little like a Spanish potato omelette. But the coriander flavours the egg and potato and makes it unmistakenly of Middle Eastern origin.

3 tablespoons olive oil
1 teaspoon ground coriander
450 g (1 lb) potatoes, peeled and finely sliced
sea salt and freshly ground black pepper
6 eggs, beaten
6 spring onions, finely chopped
3 tablespoons finely chopped parsley

Heat the oil in a thick-bottomed frying pan and add the coriander. Place the potato slices in a layer to cover the bottom of the pan, sprinkle with salt and pepper, and cook over a low flame for 15 minutes.

Mix together the eggs, spring onions and parsley, and pour over the potatoes. Cover the pan and continue to cook for another 10 minutes. Serve warm, cut into wedges, with a yoghurt sauce.

Serves 10

Chahcouka
TUNISIA
Poached eggs in pepper sauce

This method of poaching eggs is not unlike the Italian recipe for eggs poached in tomato sauce (see page 68), but here the sauce is hot with chillies and garlic. It is delicious.

4 tablespoons olive oil
4 cloves garlic, crushed
3 peppers, seeded and sliced
2 chilli peppers, seeded and sliced
450 g (1 lb) tomatoes, peeled and chopped
sea salt and freshly ground black pepper
6 eggs

Heat the oil in a frying pan and add the garlic, peppers and chilli. Cook over low heat for 15 minutes, then add the tomatoes and seasonings. Cook for another 10 minutes until the sauce is thick and rich.

Make six depressions in the sauce and drop an egg in each one. Cook until the whites are set. Eat with good crusty bread.

Serves 4 to 6

Tamarind *The dried fruit of the tamarind tree, also known as the Indian date, which has a sour, slightly fruity flavour. When it is bought dried, it should be soaked in water, the soaking liquor used in the cooking, and the seeds discarded.*

Eggs Pulusu
INDIA

This is a marvellous egg curry. Make sure that the hard-boiled eggs have been cooked gently, as the dish is a failure if the whites are leathery. The best method is to place the eggs in cold water, bring to the boil and, once the water is simmering, place a lid on the pan and turn off the heat. Leave untouched for 10 minutes. The eggs will then be perfectly cooked.

3 tablespoons corn oil
1 teaspoon ground asofoetida (see page 33)
1 teaspoon ground coriander
1 teaspoon fenugreek
4 cloves garlic, crushed
2 green chillies, seeded and sliced
1 onion, finely chopped
2 tablespoons tamarind paste
pinch of sea salt
150 ml (¼ pint) water
6 hard-boiled eggs

Heat the corn oil in a pan, add the spices, garlic, chillies and onion. Sauté for a few minutes, then add the tamarind paste, sea salt and water. Simmer gently for another few minutes.

Peel and slice the hard-boiled eggs in half. Lay them in the sauce and simmer for another 4–5 minutes, turning the eggs so that they are covered. Eat with rice or bread.

Serves 4 to 6

Eggo Faggots
KOREA

This is a favourite snack which is sold at many stalls. It might seem more trouble than it is worth, but it looks impressive as part of a first course.

4 eggs
1 tablespoon soy sauce
½ teaspoon tabasco or chilli pepper
2 teaspoons sesame oil
bunch of spring onions, trimmed

Beat the eggs with the soy, tabasco and half the sesame oil. Heat the remaining oil in a frying pan and pour in half the egg mixture. Cook lightly and, when the base is done, place the pan under a hot grill to cook the top. Drain and leave to cool Cook a second omelette in the same way and when it is cool, slice both omelettes into strips about 6 cm (2½ inches) long and 5 mm (¼ inch) wide.

Meanwhile, steam the spring onions for 10 minutes, slice the base and cut in two lengthways. Make small bundles of egg strips, then bind them with onion strips, tucking the ends underneath.

Serves 4

Kai Look Koei
THAILAND
Son-in-law eggs

This dish is not unlike the Indian Eggs Pulusu (see page 73), but the eggs are deep fried and have a particular flavour and appearance all their own, which is very appetising. The sauce is hotter than the Indian curry and I wonder if mother-in-law was intent on revenge.

2 tablespoons sesame oil
25 g (1 oz) ginger root, peeled and grated
2 green chillies, seeded and sliced
2 red chillies, seeded and sliced
2 cloves garlic, crushed
2 tablespoons soft brown sugar
85 ml (3 fl oz) sake or dry sherry
50 ml (2 fl oz) water
pinch of sea salt
corn oil for frying
6 hard-boiled eggs
spring onion or coriander leaves to garnish

Heat the sesame oil in a pan and sauté the grated ginger root for 1 minute, then add the chillies and garlic. Cook for another minute, then throw in the sugar with the sake or dry sherry and water, and stir until the sugar melts into the oil to make a sticky sauce. Season with salt.

Meanwhile, heat the corn oil in a wok. Peel the eggs and slice them in half. Deep fry them until they are brown and blistered. Drain on kitchen paper and arrange them on a serving dish. Cover with the hot sauce and garnish with either chopped spring onion or coriander leaves. Eat hot or cold.

Serves 4 to 6

Iritsukedofu
JAPAN
Egg and tofu omelette

Tofu does not appear very often in this book, but here the tofu is smoked. It is mixed in with the omelette, which is flavoured with sake and soy. I think it works beautifully.

2 tablespoons sesame oil
120 g (4 oz) smoked tofu, diced (see page 36)
1 tablespoon sake
3 tablespoons light soy sauce
4 eggs, beaten

Heat the sesame oil in a shallow pan and throw in the diced tofu. Fry lightly, then add the sake. Pour the soy sauce into the beaten eggs and mix thoroughly. Pour the eggs over the tofu and let the eggs set.

When the bottom is done, place the pan briefly under a hot grill so that the egg is just cooked. Slice the omelette like a cake. Eat hot or cold.

Serves 4

Dadar Djawa
JAVA
Spiced omelette

This omelette uses that thick, sweet soy sauce which is popular in Java. I use a mixture of soy and brown sugar, the sweetness of which offsets the hot chillies.

2 tablespoons peanut oil
1 onion, finely chopped
3 dried red chillies, broken
6 eggs, beaten
2 tablespoons soy sauce
1 teaspoon brown sugar
sea salt

Heat half the oil in a pan and fry the onion and chillies until soft. Add these to the beaten eggs, along with the soy sauce, sugar and salt. Heat the remaining oil in a pan and, dividing the mixture into three, cook the omelettes until they are set.

Serves 3 to 6

Huevos a la Mexicana
MEXICO
Mexican scrambled eggs

I cannot resist including this typical Mexican recipe, which is another one that uses chillies. It is a little like a very hot spiced piperade (see page 66).

2 tablespoons olive oil
25 g (1 oz) butter
2 green chillies, seeded and sliced
2 red chillies, seeded and sliced
1 small onion, finely sliced
120 g (4 oz) tomatoes, peeled and chopped
pinch of sea salt
6 eggs, beaten

Heat together the oil and butter in a pan, add the chillies and onion. Cook for a moment until soft, then add the tomatoes and salt. Cook for 3 minutes, until the tomatoes begin to make a sauce. Pour in the eggs and beat the mixture until the eggs are set.

Serves 4 to 6

PANCAKES
AND
DUMPLINGS

'We could not lead a pleasant life,
And 'twould would be finished soon,
If peas were eaten with the knife,
And gravy with the spoon.
Eat slowly: only men in rags
And gluttons old in sin,
Mistake themselves for carpet bags
And tumble victuals in'
Sir Walter Raleigh, Stans Puer ad Mensam (1861–1922)

'In eating, a third of the stomach should be filled with food, a third
with drink, and the rest left empty.' The Talmud 200

These dishes, which appear the world over in some form or other, are the cousins and offspring of breads and grains. The one thing that all nationalities and all ages have in common is that they find these foods to be one of the most delicious.

Pancakes or crêpes have been known in western Europe since the Middle Ages, and Chaucer refers to them as 'cresp' or 'crisps'. In the Far East, wafer-thin pancakes are traditionally used to wrap food which is then dipped into a sauce, they go back much further in time. They are still enjoyed today in one of the most popular Chinese dishes, Peking Duck. The Chinese are famous too for their dumplings, *dim sum*. I have not included these here as they are often flavoured with meat or shellfish.

Unleavened flat bread and pancakes are very close relatives indeed, and all the hot countries that make the former, not surprisingly, have various forms of the latter too. Pancake recipes can, of course, be made from all types of flour, with added milk, egg, cheese or vegetables. And excellent they all are.

Boxty
IRELAND

There are, as one would expect, great potato dishes in Ireland. This is one of them, which uses raw, grated potato, a central European tradition. It is a marvellous accompaniment to poached or fried eggs.

225 g (8 oz) raw potatoes, grated
225 g (8 oz) mashed potatoes
1 onion, grated
1 egg, beaten
2 tablespoons plain flour, sifted
50 g (2 oz) butter, melted
sea salt and freshly ground black pepper

Mix all the ingredients together thoroughly. Drop spoonfuls into hot oil and cook on both sides until crisp and brown.

Serves 4 to 6

Crêpes de Mais
FRANCE
Corn pancakes

The crêpes of France are justly famous: paper-thin envelopes which can encase all kinds of delicacies. This is an unusual recipe, because it has sweetcorn in it and they are more like the corn fritters so popular in America, but these are a lighter variety.

2 tablespoons plain flour, sifted
½ teaspoon cream of tartar
½ teaspoon bicarbonate of soda
sea salt and freshly ground black pepper
2 eggs, beaten
50 g (2 oz) butter, melted
1 x 200 g (7 oz) can sweetcorn, drained
3 tablespoons finely chopped parsley

Mix together the flour, raising agents and seasonings. Then add all the other ingredients, and mix thoroughly.

Drop spoonfuls of the mixture into hot oil. Cook on both sides until brown and crisp.

Serves 4 to 6

Kartoffelpuffer
GERMANY
Potato pancakes

This is a central European version of the raw, grated potato pancake. This one is flavoured with juniper berries, which makes these small pancakes extra delicious.

1 kg (2 lb) potatoes, peeled
sea salt and freshly ground black pepper
1 tablespoon juniper berries, crushed
25 g (1 oz) butter
2 tablespoons olive oil

Grate the raw potatoes into a bowl. Then add the sea salt, black pepper, and roughly crushed juniper berries. Mix well.

Melt the butter with the oil in a pan and drop spoonfuls of the potato mixture into it, smoothing the tops down so that they look like small, thick pancakes. Cook until the underside is well done, then turn them over and cook the other side.

Serves 4 to 6

Melboller
DENMARK
Green pea dumplings

Green peas make a marvellous purée by themselves. In this recipe, they are mixed with the other ingredients and used to flavour the dumplings.

225 g (8 oz) peas, fresh or frozen
1 egg
150 ml (¼ pint) water
50 g (2 oz) butter
50 g (2 oz) plain flour
sea salt and freshly ground black pepper

Cook the peas until tender. Drain well and reduce to a purée with the egg in a food processor. Reserve. Heat the water in a pan, melt the butter in it and throw in the flour, stirring energetically until a paste has formed. Leave to cool a little, then beat in the pea and egg mixture and seasonings.

Form the mixture into small dumplings using a teaspoon, and drop into boiling stock. Simmer until they puff up and float to the surface.

Makes 12

Canelones de Legumbres
SPAIN
Vegetable crêpes

This recipe owes something to the traditional light French crêpe but the filling is definitely Spanish. Manchego cheese is a hard Spanish cheese made from ewe's milk.

120 g (4 oz) plain flour, sifted
100 ml (3½ fl oz) milk
100 ml (3½ fl oz) water
1 egg, beaten
½ teaspoon salt
3 tablespoons melted butter
Filling:
3 small carrots, grated
2 small onions, grated
2 tablespoons olive oil
2 sweet dried peppers, finely sliced
2 green chillies, finely sliced
3 cloves garlic, crushed
120 g (4 oz) manchego cheese, grated

Mix together all the batter ingredients and leave to stand for 1 hour. Make the crêpes and keep warm.

To make the filling, blanch the carrots and onions for 3–4 minutes. Drain well. Heat the oil in a pan and throw in the peppers, chillies and garlic, cook for a few minutes, then add the carrots and onions. Cook for another minute, then add the grated cheese.

Fill each crêpe with some of the mixture, fold like an envelope and sprinkle the top with more cheese. Bake in a preheated oven, at 180°C (350°F), Gas Mark 4, for 5 minutes.

Serves 4–6

Knockerl
AUSTRIA
Bread dumplings

These remind me of Saltzburg, where they are served with the soup. I remember being there as a student and being so poor that I lived off soup and bread dumplings. Later, I had a play performed at the Festival and I was fêted and dined, quite often not eating as well as when I was a student and dined on delicious country soups.

25 g (1 oz) butter
120 g (4 oz) dried bread, sliced
2 eggs, beaten
150 ml (¼ pint) milk
75 g (3 oz) plain flour, sifted
sea salt and freshly ground black pepper
3 tablespoons finely chopped parsley

Melt the butter in a pan and lightly fry the slices of bread. Add the beaten eggs and milk to the flour in a bowl to make a smooth batter. Then throw in the bread and add the seasonings and parsley. Allow to stand for 1 hour.

Fill a large saucepan with salted water and bring to the boil. Throw in small portions of the mixture and let them simmer for 10 minutes or until they rise to the surface. Use in soup.

Makes 12

Crespelle di Funghi
ITALY
Mushroom pancakes

This stuffed pancake recipe uses fungi, which are available dried in Italian delicatessens.

Crêpes:
120 g (4 oz) plain flour, sifted
pinch of sea salt and freshly ground black pepper
3 eggs, beaten
25 g (1 oz) butter, melted
300 ml (½ pint) milk
butter for cooking
Filling:
25 g (1 oz) butter
8 g (¼ oz) dried fungi, soaked overnight
1 onion, finely chopped
175 g (6 oz) ricotta cheese (see page 61)
generous handful of parsley
sea salt and freshly ground black pepper
50 g (2 oz) Parmesan cheese, grated

Season the flour and beat in the eggs, butter and milk. Leave for 1 hour, then beat again. Melt a little butter and add generous spoonfuls of the batter. Cook both sides and drain on greaseproof paper.

Meanwhile, make the filling. Melt the butter in a pan. Drain the fungi and fry gently in the butter with the onion for about 4 minutes or until soft. Transfer the mixture to a bowl and mix in the ricotta cheese and parsley. Season to taste.

Fill each crêpe with a little of the stuffing. Fold like an envelope and sprinkle with grated Parmesan. Bake in a preheated oven, at 180°C (350°F), Gas Mark 4, for about 5 minutes.

Serves 4 to 6

Gnocchi de Semolino
ITALY
Small semolina dumplings

I have broken one of my own rules by including another Italian recipe, simply because this chapter would not be complete without gnocchi which are probably the best dumplings in the world. They should be very light and soft on the palate. If they are at all heavy, the cook has failed.

600 ml (1 pint) milk
225 g (8 oz) semolina
50 g (2 oz) butter
2 eggs, beaten
sea salt and freshly ground black pepper
50 g (2 oz) Parmesan cheese, grated

Slowly bring the milk to the boil and stir in the semolina. Cook slowly over low heat for about 20 minutes until the mixture becomes thick. Allow to cool a little and stir the butter into the mixture, then beat in the eggs and seasonings. Pour into a shallow dish and allow to get quite cold.

Cut into small squares. Butter a gratin dish and lay the gnocchi in it. Sprinkle liberally with grated Parmesan and place under a hot grill until bubbling and slightly brown.

Makes 20

Buckwheat flour *A strong, light, savoury flour made from roasted buckwheat and used for pancakes, thin crisp cakes, Russian blinis and Japanese noodles. Despite its name, buckwheat is not in fact a cereal but a member of the rhubarb family. The unroasted grains, which are greenish in colour, can also be used in casserole dishes.*

Blinis
RUSSIA

This is one of the great classic Russian recipes. Traditionally, blinis are eaten with caviar and soured cream, but they can be eaten with any sweet or savoury filling. The buckwheat flour gives the blinis a deliciously dark flavour, not unlike that of rye.

25 g (1 oz) dried yeast
200 g (7 oz) buckwheat flour, sifted
200 ml (7 fl oz) tepid water
200 ml (7 fl oz) milk
2 eggs, separated
½ teaspoon salt
25 g (1 oz) melted butter

Add the yeast to the flour and stir in the water, milk, egg yolks, salt and melted butter. Mix thoroughly, then cover and leave for 1 hour. Whip the egg whites until stiff and fold them into the batter. Leave for another 30 minutes.

Very lightly oil a heavy-based pan and cook spoonfuls of the batter for about 1 minute on each side. Stack the cooked blini and cover to keep warm.

Makes 12

Avocado Masial
MALABAR, INDIA
Curried avocado

This is an unusual recipe which can be used as a filling with any of the Indian pancakes, or eaten with either of the two recipes that follow.

2 large, ripe avocados, peeled and stoned
zest and juice of 2 limes
few chopped coriander leaves
2 tablespoons sesame oil
1 tablespoon mustard seeds
4 cloves garlic, finely chopped
1 small onion, finely chopped
2 green chillies, finely chopped
1 tablespoon homemade Curry Powder (see page 88)
sea salt

Cut the avocado flesh into slices, pour over the lime zest and juice, and sprinkle with some of the coriander leaves. Set aside.

Heat the oil in a pan and add the mustard seeds, garlic, onion and chillies. Fry gently for a few minutes or until the onion is softened and the seeds have popped, then stir in the curry powder and cook for another minute.

Finally, add the avocado slices and turn off the heat (avocado can heat but must not cook). Turn the avocado in the curry sauce, then serve. Sprinkle with a few more coriander leaves and a little salt.

Serves 4 to 6

Curry Powder
SOUTHERN INDIA

Chick Pea Pancakes
INDIA

Curry mixes come in all shades of flavour. This is fragrant yet mild, heat being controlled by the amount of chillies, and is much used for vegetable dishes in southern India. All the spices must be lightly roasted before being ground, so as to release their flavours.

50 g (2 oz) coriander seeds
50 g (2 oz) cumin seeds
50 g (2 oz) mustard seeds
50 g (2 oz) fenugreek
50 g (2 oz) black peppercorns
2–3 red chillies
3 tablespoons turmeric powder
2 tablespoons asofoetida (see page 33)

Grind the coriander, cumin, mustard, fenugreek, peppercorns and chillies to a fine powder, then add the turmeric and asofoetida. Store in an airtight container.

Makes 275 g (10 oz)

There are many recipes from India which are varieties of pancakes made from this flour. This one also includes whole chickpeas in it, which give the pancake an interesting texture.

120 g (4 oz) gram flour, sifted (see page 16)
½ teaspoon sea salt
½ teaspoon turmeric
pinch of cayenne pepper
pinch of fenugreek
1 egg, beaten
300 ml (½ pint) water
vegetable oil for frying
75 g (3 oz) chick peas, cooked

Mix the gram flour with the salt and spices. Add the beaten egg and make a paste. Slowly add the water and beat thoroughly to make a batter.

Oil a pan and pour a quarter of the batter into it. Scatter some chick peas over the surface and let the pancake cook slowly for about 6 minutes. When the underside is done, turn the pancake over and quickly finish the cooking.

Makes 10

Masala Vada
SOUTHERN INDIA
Split pea pancakes

This is a recipe, from the vegetarian part of the sub-continent, which is made from another delicious flour — that made of split peas. You can buy this in good grocers or make your own from grinding split peas in the food processor. These pancakes also include cooked split peas as well as many spices, and are very delicious.

½ teaspoon cream of tartar
½ teaspoon bicarbonate of soda
300 ml (½ pint) water
175 g (6 oz) split pea flour
75 g (3 oz) split peas, cooked
1 onion, grated
3 green chillies, seeded and sliced
3 red chillies, seeded and sliced
50 g (2 oz) ginger root, peeled and grated
½ teaspoon sea salt
corn oil for frying

Add the raising agents and water to the split pea flour. Beat to a smooth batter. Then add the cooked split peas, onion, spices and salt, and allow to stand for 1 hour.

Cook spoonfuls of the mixture in hot corn oil for about 5–6 minutes each side, until brown and crisp.

Makes 15

Split pea flour *Flour made, as the name says, from dried and ground yellow split peas.*

Yeshimba Asa
ETHIOPIA
Spiced dumplings

This is chick pea dough which is first fried and then poached in a very hot sauce.

Dough:
225 g (8 oz) gram flour, sifted (see page 16)
pinch of sea salt
100 ml (3½ fl oz) warm water
corn oil for frying
Sauce:
85 ml (3 fl oz) corn oil
2 large onions, finely sliced
5 cloves garlic, finely sliced
50 g (2 oz) ginger root, finely grated
½ teaspoon ground cloves
½ teaspoon ground cinnamon
½ teaspoon ground ginger
1 tablespoon cayenne pepper
pinch of sea salt
150 ml (¼ pint) water

Season the flour with the salt and add enough water to the flour to make a thick dough. Leave it to rest for 30 minutes, then roll it out and cut into small shapes. Leave to rest again, covered, for 10 minutes.

Meanwhile, make the sauce. Heat the oil in a pan and gently fry the onions, garlic and ginger root in it until the onions are soft. Add all the spices and the salt. Cook for a few more minutes, then add the water and simmer for 5 more minutes.

Heat the oil and fry the pieces of dough until crisp. Then drop them into the sauce and cook for a few minutes more. Serve with a little sauce.

Makes 12

Oyster Mushrooms with Sesame and Coriander
THAILAND

This recipe is often used as a filling for pancakes but is equally delicious on its own. If it is to be eaten with pancakes, use the chick pea flour mix for Sabzi Pakoda from Bangladesh (see page 92) without the vegetables.

2 tablespoons sesame oil
225 g (8 oz) oyster mushrooms
1 tablespoon sesame seeds, roasted
a few coriander leaves, chopped
juice of 1 lemon

Heat the sesame oil in a pan and throw in the mushrooms. Cook for a few minutes until they are just beginning to contract and soften. Pour on to a serving platter, sprinkle with sesame seeds and coriander. Finally, squeeze over the lemon juice.

Serves 4 to 6

Sabzi Pakoda
BANGLADESH
Vegetable fritters

These individual fritters are rich in spices and vegetables and also include a raising agent so that they puff up in cooking.

175 g (6 oz) gram flour, sifted (see page 16)
½ teaspoon cream of tartar
½ teaspoon bicarbonate of soda
½ teaspoon ground cumin
½ teaspoon ground coriander
½ teaspoon mustard seeds
½ teaspoon garam masala
½ teaspoon sea salt
300 ml (½ pint) water
2 green chillies, finely chopped
3 tablespoons corn oil
1 small aubergine, chopped
1 onion, sliced

Mix together the flour, raising agents, spices and salt, then slowly beat in the water and add the chillies. Heat the oil in a pan and fry the aubergine and onion until soft. When cool, add these to the batter. Beat again thoroughly and fry spoonfuls of the mixture in hot oil on both sides until brown and crisp.

Makes 12

Garam masala *A mixture of various aromatic spices, such as cardamom, coriander, cumin, chilli and black pepper, which can be bought ready-made.*

Hoppers
SRI LANKA

This recipe, with curiously anglicised name, derives from the colonial settlements of the nineteenth century and I suspect it was an attempt by the English to make a kind of crumpet or muffin. That notwithstanding, it is actually very good.

175 g (6 oz) plain flour, sifted
50 g (2 oz) rice flour, sifted
15 g (½ oz) dried yeast
1 teaspoon sea salt
250 ml (8 fl oz) coconut milk
vegetable oil for frying

Mix together all the ingredients and allow to stand for 1 hour. Heat a wok with a little oil smeared on it, drop in a spoonful of the mixture, swirl it around then leave to set so that the top edge is a little thinner than the bottom one and is curling and slightly brown. Turn out on to a plate. Eat with a hot sauce.

Makes 10

K'u Kua Tou Shih
CHINA
Bitter melon with salted black beans

Bitter melon may be difficult to find here, in which case you should use butternut squash which is now available in some supermarkets. Salted black beans can be bought easily in Chinese grocers. This is another recipe for a pancake stuffing. Use the Bangladesh pancake mix as in Sabzi Pakoda (see opposite) without the vegetables.

1 small bitter melon or butternut squash, peeled and seeded
4 tablespoons peanut oil
225 g (8 oz) salted black beans (see page 104)
1 teaspoon sugar
1 teaspoon sea salt
85 ml (3 fl oz) dry sherry or rice wine
2 tablespoons shoyu sauce
spring onions to garnish

Cut the melon or squash into slices. Heat the oil in a wok, throw in the melon or squash and stir fry for 2–3 minutes. Add the salted black beans, sugar, salt, sherry and shoyu, and stir fry for another minute or so. Serve at once, garnished with a few strips of spring onions.

Serves 4 to 6

Bitter melon and butternut squash *These are part of a very large family of marrows, squashes and gourds, which also includes the better-known courgettes and pumpkins. They have a rather watery, bland taste. Some are available in the winter, and all in the summer and autumn.*

Bullas
JAMAICA
Baked spiced dumplings

This West Indian recipe sometimes appears in small cakes, which have sugar added to them and are eaten with a dessert. This is the savoury version, which is eaten as a kind of bread or poached in soup.

25 g (1 oz) root ginger, grated
50 g (2 oz) butter
450 g (1 lb) plain flour, sifted
1 teaspoon cream of tartar
1 teaspoon bicarbonate of soda
1 teaspoon sea salt
1 tablespoon sweet pimento powder
1 teaspoon hot pimento powder
250 ml (8 fl oz) water

Fry the ginger gently in the butter. Mix all the dry ingredients together, then add the buttery ginger and water. Knead to a firm and pliable consistency, then leave to rest for 1 hour.

Roll out on a floured board to about 1 cm (½ inch) in thickness. Cut out small circles and place on a baking sheet. Bake in a preheated oven, at 190°C (375°F), Gas Mark 5, for 30 minutes. Eat with soup, or poach them in the soup for a moment before serving.

Makes 20

Shoyu *Pure soya sauce made with soya beans, salt and wheat or barley. It is slightly salty and can be used as a flavouring instead of salt.*

STEWS
AND
CASSEROLES

*'Cauliflower is nothing but cabbage with a
college education.'*
Mark Twain

*'The pleasure of eating is
the only one which, enjoyed in moderation,
is not followed by weariness.'*
Jean-Anthelme Brillat-Savarin,
La Physiologie du goût, 1825

Stews and casseroles are one-pot meals and perhaps one of the oldest dishes known to us. The pot was hung over the fire. The foods that were at hand were cooked in it with water and herbs. The meal was eaten with bread, which was used to soak up the juices.

True vegetarian one-pot meals are not as common as those which are made up of vegetables and meat or, as in poorer families, where just the bones would have been used. Vegetable stews are, in fact, a relative newcomer to world cuisine. Some vegetables need long slow cooking to bring out their essential qualities.

Vegetable stews are greatly enriched by a well-chosen cooking medium. Choose, for example, olive or sesame oil or butter, and flavour the liquor in which they are cooked with cider, beer, wine or strong stock, and with various herbs or spices.

Alcachofas con Piñones
SPAIN
Artichoke stew with pine nuts

Alas, we do not often get the opportunity to buy baby artichokes. It is a great shame that they are not more often available but, if you do see some, I urge you to make this stew which is fairly common in Spain. I am afraid that tinned artichokes will not do as a substitute. The pine nuts used in the cooking here were an inheritance from their Moorish conquerors.

85 ml (3 fl oz) olive oil
3 onions, sliced
1 head of garlic cloves, chopped
25 small artichokes, trimmed and halved
1 tablespoon oregano
2 x 400 g (14 oz) cans tomatoes
sea salt and freshly ground black pepper
50 g (2 oz) pine nuts

Heat the olive oil in a large pan, then throw in the onions, garlic, artichokes and oregano. Sauté for 3 minutes before adding the tomatoes. Simmer for 30 minutes then season with salt and pepper. Roast the pine nuts in a dry pan until golden, scatter them over the stew and serve.

Serves 8 to 10

Chou Rouge Braisé aux Marrons
FRANCE

Braised red cabbage with chestnuts

There are many red cabbage casseroles from central and eastern Europe, some of which use fruit to lighten the flavour. This one from France is a wonderful stew which marries two flavours beautifully. Red cabbage always benefits by long, slow cooking and the chestnuts add much in both flavour and texture.

85 ml (3 fl oz) olive oil
1.5 kg (3 lb) cabbage, chopped
450 g (1 lb) chestnuts, peeled and chopped
1 head of garlic cloves, chopped
1 onion, chopped
250 ml (8 fl oz) red wine
sea salt and freshly ground black pepper

Pour the olive oil into a large casserole and throw in the cabbage, chestnuts, garlic and onion. Sauté for a few minutes, then pour in the wine and season. Bring to a simmer, then place in a preheated oven, at 180°C (350°F), or Gas Mark 4, for 2 hours.

Serves 8 to 10

Bauernspeise
GERMANY
Cabbage and potato stew

This is a typical central European stew, with its heady aroma of pickled cabbage. You can buy bottles of ready-made sauerkraut in delicatessens now and it is well worth trying this recipe.

85 ml (3 fl oz) olive oil
225 g (8 oz) sauerkraut
1 small cabbage, chopped
2 onions, sliced
3 cloves garlic, chopped
2 bay leaves
½ teaspoon caraway seeds
1 tablespoon paprika
450 g (1 lb) potatoes, peeled and diced
300 ml (½ pint) dry cider
pinch of sea salt

Heat the olive oil in a large pan, then add the sauerkraut, cabbage, onions, garlic, bay leaves and spices. Sauté for 5 minutes, then add the potatoes, cider and salt. Place a lid on the pan and simmer for 20 minutes.

Serves 4 to 6

Fèves à la Poulette
CORSICA
Broad beans in cream

Both on the Corsican island and further south in Sardinia, broad beans are a favourite food, ripening early in spring, and are generally eaten raw from the pod. This recipe, which uses a thick cream sauce flecked with parsley, is cooked when the broad beans are mature, though the inner bean will always have to be shelled.

1 kg (2 lb) broad beans, shelled
25 g (1 oz) butter
1 teaspoon flour
sea salt and freshly ground black pepper
2 egg yolks
1 tablespoon thick cream
2 tablespoons chopped parsley

Cook the broad beans in a little boiling water for about 8 minutes. Strain, but reserve about 150 ml (¼ pint) of the cooking liquor.

Melt the butter in a pan, stir in the flour and cook for a moment, then add the reserved cooking water. Season with salt and freshly ground black pepper, and add the beans to the sauce. Let them cook for 2–3 minutes. Stir in the egg yolks and then the cream. Let the sauce thicken, then sprinkle with chopped parsley.

Serves 4 to 6

Kounoupithi Kapama
GREECE
Cauliflower casserole

You will often see this casserole in Greek taverna kitchens. Never overcook the cauliflower which should always be al dente, when it can also be eaten cold as a salad.

1 large cauliflower
50 g (2 oz) butter
1 onion, sliced
2 cloves garlic, crushed
juice and zest of 1 lemon
150 ml (¼ pint) water
3 tablespoons tomato purée
sea salt and freshly ground black pepper
2 tablespoons chopped parsley to garnish

Break the cauliflower into individual florets. Melt the butter in a casserole dish and cook the onion and garlic until soft. Mix together the lemon juice and zest, water and tomato purée to make a smooth sauce.

Season with salt and pepper then add the cauliflower, spooning the sauce over each piece. Place the lid on the casserole dish and simmer for about 5 minutes. Sprinkle the parsley over the dish and serve.

Serves 4 to 6

Zelyoni
RUSSIA
Green stew

This vegetable stew is characteristically flavoured with dill and eaten with soured cream. Do not be mean with the dill.

50 g (2 oz) butter
50 ml (2 fl oz) olive oil
450 g (1 lb) baby carrots, trimmed and chopped
225 g (8 oz) turnips, trimmed and chopped
2 large onions, chopped
2 tablespoons dill weed (see page 71)
450 g (1 lb) potatoes, peeled and chopped
450 g (1 lb) spinach, washed and chopped small
1 small cabbage, trimmed and sliced
1.25 litres (2¼ pints) strong vegetable stock
150 ml (¼ pint) dry white wine
sea salt and freshly ground black pepper
150 ml (¼ pint) soured cream

Melt the butter with the olive oil in a large saucepan. Throw in the carrots, turnips, onions and dill weed. Sauté for moment, then add the potatoes, spinach and cabbage.

Continue to cook over a low flame for about 5 minutes, then add the stock. Bring to the boil and simmer for 15 minutes. Then add the dry white wine and season to taste with salt and pepper. Simmer for another 15 minutes, then stir in the soured cream just before serving.

Serves 8 to 10

Letcho
HUNGARY
Pepper and tomato stew

This is a little like the French piperade (see page 66) but without the eggs. It is given its distinctive flavour by the amount of green peppers used and the addition of hot paprika.

50 ml (2 fl oz) olive oil
6 medium green peppers, seeded and sliced
2 onions, sliced
1 head of garlic cloves, chopped
1 tablespoon hot paprika
sea salt
2 x 400 g (14 oz) cans tomatoes

Heat the olive oil in a large pan, throw in the peppers, onions and garlic. Sauté for a moment, then stir in the paprika and salt.

Lastly, add the tomatoes, bring to the boil and simmer for 20 minutes. By this time, the sauce should have reduced a little and thickened.

Serves 4 to 6

Turlu
TURKEY
Mixed vegetable stew

This bean and vegetable stew from Turkey is very like some of the Greek recipes, but then that's hardly surprising because their cuisine is close. It is well worth bothering about the quality of the olive oil in all these recipes.

100 ml (3½ fl oz) olive oil
2 bay leaves
1 tablespoon crushed coriander seeds
175 g (6 oz) haricot beans, soaked
3 small potatoes, peeled and chopped
2 carrots, diced
4 onions, chopped
1 head of garlic cloves, chopped
sea salt and freshly ground black pepper
generous handful of parsley, chopped

Heat the olive oil, throw in the bay leaves, coriander and drained beans. Add enough water to come 4 cm (1½ inches) above the beans and simmer for 30 minutes.

Add the rest of the vegetables and simmer for another 20 minutes. Season and stir in the parsley.

Serves 4 to 6

Bamia
EGYPT
Okra and tomato stew

Okra stews are famous from all the hot countries. This one from Egypt sometimes has added sugar in it, but if the tomatoes are ripe you will have a natural sweetness which I think is preferable.

85 ml (3 fl oz) olive oil
1 large onion, sliced
1 head of garlic cloves, chopped
750 g (1½ lb) okra, trimmed
1 tablespoon ground coriander
1 large aubergine, diced and salted for 1 hour
750 g (1½ lb) fresh tomatoes, peeled and chopped,
or 2 x 400 g (14 oz) cans
sea salt and freshly ground black pepper
3 tablespoons chopped coriander leaves

Heat the olive oil in a large casserole, throw in the onion, garlic, okra and ground coriander, and sauté for a few minutes. Rinse, drain and dry the diced aubergine and add this too.

Sauté for a few minutes more, then add the tomatoes, bring to the boil and simmer for 30 minutes. Season and stir in the coriander leaves.

Serves 8 to 10

Okra *Also called lady's fingers or gumbo, okra can be bought either fresh all year round or canned. It is the young seed pod of an African plant in the hibiscus family containing tiny edible seeds. When buying, choose small pods as these are the most tender. It is eaten as a vegetable and used to thicken stews and soups.*

Batata Bil Limoun
MOROCCO
Potato and lemon casserole

This particular combination of potato and lemon is common in all the countries of north Africa. It is a particularly delicious partnership, especially when, as here, it is spiced with red chillies.

100 ml (3½ fl oz) olive oil
2 large onions, chopped
1 head of garlic cloves, chopped
1 tablespoon ground cumin
1 tablespoon ground coriander
2 dried red chillies, broken
1 kg (2 lb) potatoes, peeled and sliced
zest and juice of 2 lemons
600 ml (1 pint) water
sea salt
generous handful of parsley, chopped, to garnish

Heat the olive oil in a large casserole, throw in the onions, garlic and spices, and sauté for a few minutes. Then add the potatoes, lemon zest and juice, water and salt. Simmer for 20 minutes.

Drain off any excess liquid. Scatter the chopped parsley over the dish before serving.

Serves 6 to 8

Su Ts'ai Tang
CHINA
Vegetable stew

This is a steaming hot vegetable stew eaten in the winter. Make sure that the sesame oil is of good quality and really flavours the stew. You can also roast and grind sesame seeds and add them at the beginning of cooking.

85 ml (3 fl oz) sesame oil
1 small cabbage, finely chopped
2 small carrots, diced
2 medium potatoes, peeled and diced
1 green pepper, cored, seeded and diced
1 red pepper, cored, seeded and diced
2 onions, sliced
120 g (4 oz) tofu, diced (see page 36)
900 ml (1½ pints) strong vegetable stock
sea salt and freshly ground black pepper

Heat the sesame oil, throw in all the vegetables and tofu, and sauté for a few minutes. Add the vegetable stock and simmer for 20 minutes.

Taste and adjust the seasoning.

Serves 4 to 6

Black beans *A member of the kidney bean family, which originated in South America and was brought to Europe by Columbus in the sixteenth century. They are big and shiny, and are now grown mainly in Thailand and China. Salted black beans, available in Chinese stores have been cooked and salted to preserve them, so they don't need cooking and will keep in a refrigerator for several months.*

Takiawase
JAPAN
Bamboo shoot stew

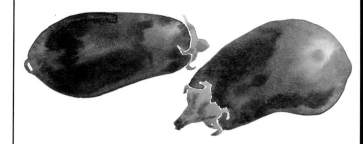

You can buy cans of bamboo shoots in good delicatessen shops and this stew flavoured with salted black beans and garlic is particularly good in the winter. For extra warmth, add a little more sherry or sake just before serving.

50 ml (2 fl oz) corn oil
450 g (1 lb) mushrooms, sliced
1 x 400 g (14 oz) can bamboo shoots, sliced
2 cloves garlic, sliced
120 g (4 oz) salted black beans
225 g (8 oz) bean sprouts
85 ml (3 fl oz) soy sauce
85 ml (3 fl oz) dry sherry or sake
few leaves of watercress to garnish

Heat the corn oil in a pan, throw in the mushrooms, bamboo shoots and garlic, and sauté until the mushrooms are soft. Add the black beans, bean sprouts, soy and sherry or sake. Simmer for 2–3 minutes before serving.

Garnish with a few leaves of watercress.

Serves 4 to 6

Pinakbet
PHILIPPINES
Mixed vegetable stew

This is another okra stew, but this one is given a particular flavour by the use of the bitter gourd. These are available more readily now in our vegetable markets and are one of the large squash, marrow and gourd family.

2 small aubergines, cut in strips and salted for 1 hour
1 bitter gourd, seeded, cut in strips and salted for 1 hour
50 ml (2 fl oz) corn oil
50 g (2 oz) ginger root, peeled and grated
5 cloves garlic, chopped
1 large onion, chopped
225 g (8 oz) okra, trimmed and washed (see page 103)
225 g (8 oz) green beans
225 g (8 oz) broad beans
1 x 400 g (14 oz) can tomatoes
85 ml (3 fl oz) dark soy sauce
sea salt and freshly ground black pepper

Rinse the pieces of aubergine and bitter gourd and pat dry. Heat the corn oil in a large casserole, throw in the ginger, garlic and onion, and sauté for a moment before adding the vegetables, tomatoes, soy and seasonings.

Cook for 15–20 minutes, or until the sauce has reduced and thickened a little.

Serves 6 to 8

Crema de Elote
MEXICO
Corn chowder

We associate chowders with America, but this recipe comes from further south and has been deliciously spiced with green chillies and peppers. I also particularly like the way the Mexicans use their local cheese, a dry, salty goat's cheese called anejo, which is unobtainable here so I have used feta.

3 green peppers
75 g (3 oz) butter
450 g (1 lb) frozen corn niblets, thawed
1 large onion, finely sliced
3 cloves garlic, chopped
2 green chillies, seeded and sliced
150 ml (¼ pint) vegetable stock
600 ml (1 pint) milk
1 tablespoon cornflour
150 ml (¼ pint) single cream
175 g (6 oz) feta cheese, crumbled (see page 14)
sea salt
generous handful of parsley, finely chopped

Roast the peppers over a flame until they blister. Then scrape off the outer skin and cut into dice.

Melt the butter in a pan, throw in the corn, onion, garlic and chillies, and sauté gently for a moment before adding the vegetable stock. Continue to simmer for 10 minutes.

Mix the milk with the cornflour and add this to the vegetables. Wait until it thickens, then add the cream, feta and diced green peppers. Season to taste with salt and add the parsley. Bring to simmering point before serving.

Serves 4 to 6

PASTA, PULSE AND GRAIN DISHES

'There will be no beans in the Almost Perfect State.'
Don Marquis

'In no department of life, in no place, should indifference be allowed
to creep; into none less than the
domain of cookery.'
Yuan Mei q. in Food *by Waverley Root, 1980*

These dishes are prolific. Grains, which are the most basic food as we have seen in the bread section, are refined into pasta as in Italy, or are left much as they are in the burghuls of the Middle East. These grain dishes, I'm happy to say, are gaining popularity, and are an excellent substitute for rice in a hot dish or as a summer salad with lemon, mint and oil.

In this chapter, there are also a few pulse dishes. Grains and pulses are complementary proteins, one supplying the amino acids the other lacks, so it is sensible to eat a dish of each in the same meal or within a few hours of each other, as this will boost the nutritional value of both foods.

<u>Arroz con Azafran</u>
SPAIN
Saffron rice

Saffron *The English word 'saffron' is derived from the Arab 'Za faran', which means yellow. The planting and harvesting are still done by hand. The harvesting lasts for only ten days and a pound of saffron is composed of 225,000 stigmas of 75,000 flowers from the saffron crocus. Given all that, it's hardly surprising that it's said to be the most expensive spice in the world!*

The Arabs introduced saffron to Spain in the eighth century. It came to England in the Middle Ages when Saffron Walden became the centre of the saffron industry. The colour of the strands should be a vibrant orange red, with an aromatic bouquet, very pronounced in the cooking.

25 g (1 oz) butter
50 ml (2 fl oz) olive oil
5 cloves garlic, chopped
1 onion, chopped
350 g (12 oz) patna rice
750 ml (1¼ pints) strong vegetable stock
1 teaspoon saffron threads

Heat the butter with the olive oil and add the garlic and onion,. Fry gently for a few minutes until they are soft. Then throw in the rice, stir and let the rice soak up the flavours.

Heat the stock with the saffron and pour over the rice. Cover the pan and simmer for 6–8 minutes or until the rice is cooked but still al dente.

Serves 4 to 6

Kroketes me Ryzi
GREECE
Rice croquettes

These croquettes are so highly flavoured that, if they are small enough, they can persuade the unsophisticated diner that he or she is eating Greek meat balls. Make sure that you fry them well, so that they are thoroughly crisp on the outside.

350 g (12 oz) brown rice
900 ml (1½ pints) water
120 g (4 oz) feta cheese (see page 14)
50 g (2 oz) pine nuts
2 teaspoons dried oregano
5 cloves garlic, crushed
1 onion, finely chopped
3 eggs, separated
2 tablespoons finely chopped parsley
sea salt and freshly ground black pepper
50 g (2 oz) wholemeal flour
50 g (2 oz) wholemeal breadcrumbs
corn oil for frying

Cook the rice in the water. When the rice is done, add the feta, pine nuts, oregano, garlic and onion. Stir well to mix thoroughly.

Add the egg yolks to the rice. Now add the chopped parsley and seasonings, and form into small cakes the size of a golf ball. Roll them first in flour, then in egg white, and then in breadcrumbs, and fry in corn oil for about 4 minutes until crisp and brown.

Makes 20

Spaghetti Alla Puttanesca
ITALY
Spaghetti with olives, capers and tomatoes

I believe that the simpler the recipe for spaghetti and its sauces, the more successful it is. The simplest of all, perhaps, is spaghetti tossed in olive oil and raw chopped garlic, which is a superb Neapolitan recipe. This one, which includes tomatoes, olives and capers, is perhaps even better and I think it has now become my favourite spaghetti recipe.

150 ml (¼ pint) olive oil
75 g (3 oz) butter
450 g (1 lb) tomatoes, quartered
6 cloves garlic
4 tablespoons capers
sea salt and freshly ground black pepper
75 g (3 oz) black olives, pitted and halved
350 g (12 oz) spaghetti
3 tablespoons finely chopped parsley to garnish

Heat the olive oil and butter in a large frying pan, add the tomatoes and cook these with the garlic and capers for about 5 minutes. Season with salt and pepper, and scatter the olives over the top.

Boil the spaghetti in plenty of salted water and, when it is al dente, drain and pour into a warm serving dish. Pour on the sauce and sprinkle with chopped parsley.

Serves 6 to 8

Lasagne Verde
ITALY
Green lasagne

I have to include another Italian recipe because this green lasagne, made with a purée of fresh peas, has become such a favourite dish of mine for parties. It will feed 12 to 15 people quite happily.

10 strips wholemeal lasagne
salt for lasagne water
butter to grease dish
1 kg (2 lb) courgettes, sliced
1 kg (2 lb) spinach
1 kg (2 lb) fresh peas, podded
300 ml (½ pint) semi-skimmed milk
2 eggs, beaten
sea salt and freshly ground black pepper
120 g (4 oz) sage Derby cheese, grated
Cheese sauce:
25 g (1 oz) butter
50 g (2 oz) plain flour
300 ml (½ pint)
semi-skimmed milk
75 g (3 oz) mature
Cheddar cheese, grated
sea salt
freshly ground
black pepper

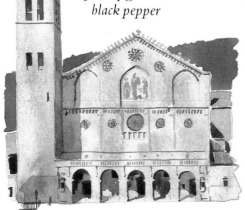

Preheat the oven to 200°C (400°F), Gas Mark 6. Boil the strips of lasagne in plenty of salted water for 10–15 minutes. When it is done, take each piece out separately and drain on tea towels. Choose a large, wide, shallow ovenproof dish. Butter it and lay two-thirds of the sheets of lasagne on the bottom and around the sides.

Cook the courgettes with the spinach in their own juices for 10–12 minutes. Chop the cooked spinach with a wooden spoon and arrange it with the courgettes over the lasagne in the dish. Cook the peas in boiling water for about 8 minutes. Drain and liquidise with the semi-skimmed milk and beaten eggs. Season with salt and pepper. Sprinkle the grated sage Derby cheese over the spinach in the dish. Pour the liquidised pea mixture over the cheese and cover with the remaining pasta sheets.

Now prepare the sauce. Make a roux with the butter and flour. Gradually add the milk, stirring all the time. Add the Cheddar cheese and season the sauce, which should be fairly thick, with salt and pepper.

Pour the sauce over the lasagne, ensuring that it is completely covered. Bake in the preheated oven for 30 minutes, or until the top is brown and the interior is bubbling.

Serves 12 to 15

Ful Medames
EGYPT
Egyptian brown beans

This is the classic Egyptian bean dish which you will find at stalls on every street corner. These beans are available in some wholefood and delicatessen shops, but if you are in the Middle East buy them there (they are very cheap) and bring them home with you.

450 g (1 lb) Egyptian brown beans, soaked overnight
5 garlic cloves, crushed
50 ml (2 fl oz) olive oil
juice and zest of 2 lemons
sea salt and freshly ground black pepper
Garnish:
3 hard-boiled eggs
generous handful of parsley, finely chopped

Drain the beans and place them in a large dish covered with plenty of water. Bring to the boil and simmer for 2 hours, when the beans should be tender but still whole. Drain the beans and add them to all the other ingredients while they are still warm. Leave the beans to rest and soak up the garlic, oil and lemon.

Shell and slice the hard-boiled eggs. Place the beans on a platter and decorate with the hard-boiled eggs. Finally, sprinkle with chopped parsley.

Serves 12

Burghul bi Dfeen
LEBANON
Cracked wheat and chick pea pilaf

There are many burghuls and pilafs from the Middle East but the ones I prefer are, like this one, a mixture of grains and pulses. That means that you are getting complementary protein.

175 g (6 oz) chick peas, soaked overnight
85 ml (3 fl oz) olive oil
2 onions, chopped
3 cloves garlic, chopped
2 teaspoons allspice
1 teaspoon ground cumin
1 teaspoon ground coriander
275 g (10 oz) cracked wheat
sea salt and freshly ground black pepper
600 ml (1 pint) vegetable stock

Cook the chick peas in plenty of water for about 1 hour. Heat the olive oil in a pan and sauté the onions and garlic with the spices for a few minutes, then add the cooked chick peas and cracked wheat. Season with salt and pepper, and add enough vegetable stock to cover by 2.5 cm (1 inch).

Allow to simmer for 6–8 minutes. Eat with yoghurt and pickles.

Serves 12

Nvig
ARMENIA
Chick peas with spinach

This, like many grain and pulse dishes, was eaten during Lent. It seems amazing that such a delicious and cunning mixture, the chick peas soaking up the spinach juices and spices, should be thought a sensory deprivation, but traditionally such dishes were eaten by the rich as an act of Lenten piety.

225 g (8 oz) chick peas, soaked overnight
sea salt and freshly ground black pepper
3 tablespoons olive oil
4 cloves garlic, crushed
450 g (1 lb) spinach, washed
3 tablespoons tomato purée
1 tablespoon ground cumin
1 tablespoon ground coriander

Boil the chick peas for 2 hours or until they are tender. Salt the water and allow them to stand while you cook the spinach.

Heat the oil in a large pan and throw in the garlic and then the spinach leaves. Simmer over low heat until the spinach is reduced to a third of its bulk. Chop it up roughly with a wooden spoon, then add the remaining ingredients, along with the drained chick peas. Season with salt and pepper, and simmer for another 10 minutes. If there is any liquor left in the pan, raise the heat and reduce to nothing.

Serves 6 to 8

Shula Kalambar
IRAN
Lentils with spinach

Spinach is a popular vegetable in the Middle East. It also goes very well with all the pulse family.

175 g (6 oz) large brown lentils
1 onion, sliced
4 cloves garlic, chopped
450 g (1 lb) fresh spinach leaves
3 tablespoons olive oil
1 teaspoon coriander seeds, roughly ground
1 teaspoon ground cumin
25 g (1 oz) butter
sea salt and freshly ground black pepper

Boil the lentils with the onion and garlic for about 15 minutes, until just tender. Cook the spinach in its own juice until reduced to a third of its bulk. Drain off any excess liquid.

Heat the olive oil and sauté the spices for a moment, then throw in the cooked lentils and stir in the spinach. Let them cook together for a few minutes, then stir in the butter and season.

Serves 4 to 6

Lobio
RUSSIA
Red beans and walnuts

The flavours of red kidney beans and walnuts go together marvellously. This is also excellent as a bean salad.

225 g (8 oz) red kidney beans, soaked overnight
150 ml (¼ pint) olive oil
4 cloves garlic, chopped
120 g (4 oz) walnuts, roughly crushed
2 teaspoons paprika
pinch of cayenne pepper
sea salt and freshly ground black pepper

Cook the beans in plenty of boiling water for 45–60 minutes, or until tender. Drain. Heat half the olive oil, throw in half the garlic, cook for a moment then add the beans and half the walnuts. Heat together gently and season well with the paprika, cayenne, salt and pepper.

Meanwhile, put the remaining oil, garlic and walnuts in a food processor. Blend to a thick purée and, when the beans are hot, stir this in.

Serves 6 to 8

Tamatar Bhat
INDIA
Tomato pilaf

Pilafs can, of course, be made out of any vegetables, rice and flavourings but this one is subtly flavoured and is delicious as long as you use fresh coriander.

50 ml (2 fl oz) corn oil
1 large onion, finely sliced
3 cloves garlic, chopped
1 tablespoon coriander seeds, roughly ground
1 tablespoon mustard seeds
1 x 400 g (14 oz) can tomatoes
350 g (12 oz) basmati rice
sea salt and freshly ground black pepper
3 tablespoons finely chopped coriander

Heat the corn oil in a large pan, and throw in the onion, garlic, coriander and mustard seeds. Cook for a few minutes with the lid on to stop the mustard seeds popping out over the stove.

Add the tomatoes and their juices, and cook for a further 5 minutes before stirring in the rice. Add enough water to cover the rice by 1 cm (½ inch). Simmer for 15 minutes, by which time the rice should have absorbed most of the liquid. Stir in the seasonings and the finely chopped coriander leaves.

Serves 4 to 6

Chinese leaves *A type of celery cabbage from Asia and China. It looks a little like a Cos lettuce. Crunchy and tasting somewhere between celery and cabbage, it can be stir-fried or used raw in salads. Pak choi is one of the main varieties and has dark green leaves and broad white stems.*

Ts'ai Fau
CHINA
Vegetable rice

I am not over fond of Chinese leaves and prefer the purple pak choi, but this recipe seems to me to be the one which makes Chinese leaves taste good, as they are mixed with the rice and flavourings.

50 ml (2 fl oz) peanut or sesame oil
1 Chinese leaves or pak choy cabbage, sliced
450 g (1 lb) mushrooms, sliced
2 large onions, sliced
450 g (1 lb) patna rice
750 ml (1¼ pints) water
sea salt and freshly ground black pepper

Heat the oil in a large pan, and throw in the cabbage, mushrooms and onions. Sauté for 3–4 minutes until the vegetables have lost some of their moisture, then stir in the rice and let it soak up some of the flavours before adding the water.

Simmer for 6–8 minutes until the rice is cooked but still al dente. Season well.

Serves 4 to 6

Beah Yaw
BURMA
Split pea croquettes

This is very much like the Israeli falofel (see page 60), but made with split peas instead of chick peas. The flavour is also much more intense.

275 g (10 oz) split peas, soaked for 1 hour
50 ml (2 fl oz) corn oil
3 onions, chopped
3 cloves garlic, chopped
2 green chillies, seeded and sliced
1 tablespoon mustard seeds
1 tablespoon fenugreek
1 teaspoon turmeric
1 teaspoon ground coriander
sea salt
2 tablespoons split pea flour (see page 89)
1 egg, beaten

First, put the split peas in a food processor and grind into a powder. Pour into a bowl. Heat the corn oil in a pan and cook the vegetables and spices for a few minutes.

Stir the mixture into the ground split peas. Add the salt, flour and egg. Mix to a paste. Form into small cakes and fry until brown and crisp.

Makes 20

Kao Pad Prik
THAILAND
Fried chilli rice

This recipe is interesting for the way that it uses the rice as a base for the eggs. I have eaten it when the eggs are merely fried on top of the rice. Here they are stirred in until the rice is set.

50 ml (2 fl oz) sesame oil
3 green chillies, seeded and sliced
2 dried red chillies, broken
1 tablespoon red curry paste
85 ml (3 fl oz) light soy sauce
450 g (1 lb) cooked rice
3 eggs, beaten
Garnish:
spring onions
coriander leaves

Heat the oil in a wok and fry the green and red chillies briefly. Then add the curry paste and the light soy sauce, and mix thoroughly. Now add the cooked rice and stir so that all the grains of rice are covered and take the colour and flavour of the sauce.

Lastly, pour in the eggs and stir fry the rice until the eggs have set. Tip out on to a serving platter and garnish with spring onions and fresh coriander.

Serves 8 to 10

Takenoko Meshi
JAPAN
Rice and bamboo shoots

Canned bamboo shoots are available in good delicatessen shops. Drain them well before using. They have a particularly delicious and distinctive flavour of their own.

85 ml (3 fl oz) soy sauce
85 ml (3 fl oz) sake
2 x 225 g (8 oz) cans bamboo shoots, sliced
300 ml (½ pint) strong vegetable stock
450 g (1 lb) rice

Heat the soy sauce and sake in a large saucepan, and turn the slices of bamboo shoot in it for several minutes. Add the vegetable stock and cook for a few minutes more.

Add the rice and enough water to cover it by 1 cm (½ inch). Simmer until the rice is cooked but still al dente.

Serves 8 to 10

Konghamul Bab
KOREA
Rice and bean sprouts

This is a very simple dish, consisting mainly of rice and bean sprouts. What gives it its own particular flavour is the addition of tekka, which is a Japanese condiment.

50 ml (2 fl oz) sesame oil
225 g (8 oz) patna rice
2 tablespoons light soy sauce
1 tablespoon tekka
120 g (4 oz) bean sprouts

Heat the oil in a pan and throw in the rice. Stir for a moment before adding the soy, tekka, and enough water to cover the rice by 1 cm (½ inch). Simmer for 5 minutes.

Throw in the bean sprouts so that they steam on top of the rice, and leave for another 3 minutes. Stir and serve.

Serves 4 to 6

Tekka *A Japanese condiment based on seaweed, to which many spices and flavourings can be added.*

Fettucine Alfredo
AMERICA
Rich egg noodles

I have included this recipe as a kind of sensual indulgence because it is madly rich in cream and egg. A little of it goes a long way. Chopped parsley, added at the last minute, helps to cut through some of the richness. Two mouthfuls are probably enough for most people as it ups the saturated fat content alarmingly!

175 g (6 oz) fettucine
sea salt and freshly ground black pepper
2 egg yolks
75 g (3 oz) butter, melted
150 ml (¼ pint) double cream
good pinch of nutmeg
50 g (2 oz) Parmesan cheese, grated

Boil the fettucine in salted water for 10–12 minutes until cooked but al dente. Beat the egg yolks and butter into the cream. Season with nutmeg, salt and pepper, heat gently and melt half of the Parmesan cheese into the sauce.

Drain the fettucine and place in a gratin dish. Pour the sauce over the top and flash under a very hot grill so that it bubbles. Sprinkle the rest of the grated Parmesan on the top and serve as a first course.

Serves 4 to 6

Buckaroo
AMERICA
Spiced baked beans

Boston baked beans have been made famous the world over, but this recipe pre-dates them. I think this recipe is preferable as there are more spices here, but it also needs long, slow cooking.

85 ml (3 fl oz) olive oil
3 bay leaves
1 tablespoon oregano
½ teaspoon cumin seeds
½ teaspoon mustard seeds
½ teaspoon chilli powder
450 g (1 lb) haricot beans, soaked overnight
5 cloves garlic, chopped
2 onions, chopped
2 tablespoons brown sugar
1 x 400 g (14 oz) can tomatoes
600 ml (1 pint) vegetable stock (or more)
pinch of salt

Heat the oil in a large casserole and throw in the herbs and spices with the beans, garlic and onions. Sauté for a few moments, stirring all the time. Next add the sugar and tomatoes. Add the vegetable stock, and if the liquid does not cover the beans by 2.5 cm (1 inch) add more until it does.

Bake in a preheated oven, at 160°C (325°F), Gas Mark 3, for 3–4 hours. Add salt at the end of the cooking time. Check that the beans are not drying out after 1½ hours and from time to time after that.

Serves 8 to 10

Arroz a la Poblana
MEXICO
Pepper and cheese pilaf

This is an interesting pilaf from Mexico. It is a mixture of rice and corn flavoured with chillies and peppers, and is given extra substance by the addition of feta cheese.

3 tablespoons olive oil
1 onion, chopped
4 cloves garlic, chopped
1 tablespoon oregano
225 g (8 oz) basmati rice
3 green chillies, sliced and seeded
600 ml (1 pint) vegetable stock
120 g (4 oz) frozen corn niblets, thawed
3 sweet green peppers, roasted and sliced
120 g (4 oz) feta cheese (see page 14)
few sprigs of watercress to garnish

Heat the oil in a large pan and throw in the onion, garlic, oregano, rice and chillies. Stir and sauté for a few minutes. Add the vegetable stock and simmer for 6 minutes. Add the corn and green peppers. Simmer for another 6 minutes.

Then add the feta cheese and simmer for a further 4 minutes. Turn out on to a serving platter and garnish with watercress.

Serves 6 to 8

SAVOURIES
AND
SAUCES

'Cook, see all your sauces be sharp and poynant in the
palate, that they may commend you…'
Francis Beaumont & John Fletcher

'No sauce, no health, no cooking.'
Marquis de Cussy, L' Art Culinaire

Where would we be without sauces? A hunk of
fresh bread dipped in a good sauce is a meal in itself,
or at least a good start to one. When we think of
superlative cooking, it is the sauces that bequeath
greatness to the art. From the Italian agro dolce, the
provençal aioli, the simple béchamel — most basic of
all sauces, the piquant caper or the aromatic
tarragon, to a homely onion, a fiery tabasco, a fierce
mustard or a beguiling saffron sauce: the list is
endless and they all delight the taste buds and make
the salivary glands work in overdrive.

Pesto
ITALY
Basil sauce

This is one of the world's greatest sauces, and most pesto lovers insist on growing their own basil each year. If you grow enough basil, you can keep it throughout the winter by putting the leaves in a blender with lemon juice and oil and bottling it. You can then, whenever you need pesto, take out just the amount you want and add the pine nuts and Parmesan cheese at the last moment.

generous handful of basil leaves, coarsely chopped
2 cloves garlic, crushed
juice and zest of 1 lemon
150 ml (¼ pint) olive oil (or more)
50 g (2 oz) pine nuts
25 g (1 oz) Parmesan cheese, freshly grated
sea salt and freshly ground black pepper

This famous sauce can be made very easily using a food processor. Throw the basil leaves into the food processor with the garlic, lemon juice and zest. Add the oil in a thin, steady stream to make a sauce. Then add the pine nuts to thicken the sauce and finally add the Parmesan, salt and pepper.

You may need more oil, and if the Parmesan is salty you may need to go easy on the salt.

Serves 6

Salsa Romesco
SPAIN
Chilli sauce

Along with mayonnaise and pesto, this is the third great classic sauce from western Europe—not quite as famous, perhaps, as the first two, yet it deserves to be. It is, I believe, a close relative of harissa and the idea for this sauce was probably brought to Spain by the Moors.

225 g (8 oz) tomatoes, peeled and chopped
5 cloves garlic, crushed
50 g (2 oz) almonds, roasted
10 red dried chillies, seeds and stalks removed
250 ml (8 fl oz) olive oil
juice and zest of 1 lemon
85 ml (3 fl oz) dry sherry
½ teaspoon sea salt

Combine everything in the blender jar and purée to a thickish sauce.

Makes 300 ml (½ pint)

Skordalia
GREECE
Potato and garlic puree

Everyone knows taramasalata in Greece, but not many people know this simple recipe which is, of course, especially for garlic lovers. Don't try to make it in a food processor, because the force of the machine breaks up the starch and you will end up with a grey, gluey purée which is not at all pleasant.

450 g (1 lb) floury potatoes, peeled
5 cloves garlic, crushed
juice and zest of 1 lemon
2 egg yolks
150 ml (¼ pint) olive oil
sea salt and freshly ground black pepper

Boil the potatoes, mash and force them through a sieve. Add the garlic, lemon juice and zest, and stir in the egg yolks. Add the olive oil, drop by drop, until you have a thick purée. Check the seasoning.

Makes 300 ml (½ pint)

Hren So Smetanoi
RUSSIA
Horseradish and soured cream sauce

This is a very simple sauce, common in Russia and generally eaten with salted or smoked fish. It is also excellent with egg dishes.

225 g (8 oz) horseradish, finely grated
1 tablespoon white wine vinegar
½ teaspoon sea salt
150 ml (¼ pint) soured cream

Thoroughly mix together all the ingredients. Leave to rest and chill for 1 hour.

Makes 300 ml (½ pint)

Piripiri
MOZAMBIQUE
Hot sauce

Some of the finest red chillies in the world are grown in Mozambique, so it is not surprising to find this hot sauce made out of them. The sauce is used as a cooking medium for chicken, meat and shellfish. Although it is hot, it is perfectly good with crudités, and you should serve a bowl of yoghurt with them as well.

10 dried red chillies, broken up
150 ml (¼ pint) corn oil
2 onions, finely chopped
1 head of garlic cloves, crushed
2 tablespoons soft brown sugar
sea salt
generous handful of parsley, chopped

Crush the chillies to a rough powder and cook in the oil with all the other ingredients, except the parsley, until the sauce is thick, chunky and syrupy. Finally, stir in the parsley. Use as a dipping sauce.

Makes 150 ml (¼ pint)

Baba Ghanoush
TURKEY
Aubergine and tahina puree

This is one of many famous aubergine purées from the Middle East. I think this is particularly delicious, because I love the flavour of sesame. To get an authentic flavour, the aubergines should be cooked over charcoal, but it is almost as good if the outside skin is simply blistered and blackened over a gas flame or under a grill.

3 large aubergines
5 crushed cloves garlic
150 ml (¼ pint) lemon juice
½ teaspoon ground cumin
½ teaspoon ground coriander
sea salt and freshly ground black pepper
300 ml (½ pint) tahina paste

Grill the aubergines until the interior is soft and the exterior of the skin is blackened. Slice them in half and scoop out the cooked flesh.

Add all the other ingredients, keeping the tahina paste until last. For a smoother cream use an electric blender.

Serves 6

Tahina *A paste made of ground sesame seeds, which is frequently used in Middle Eastern cooking. It is not dissimilar, in both taste and texture, to a smooth peanut butter.*

Harissa
TUNISIA
Fiery chilli sauce

This sauce from north Africa is for those people who love hot spicy food. It is traditionally added to soups and served with couscous.

120 g (4 oz) dried red chillies
4 tablespoons water
1 head of garlic cloves, crushed
1 teaspoon ground caraway seeds
1 tablespoon salt

Cut the stalks off the chillies, then soak them in the water for 1 hour. Pour into a food processor, add all the other ingredients, and blend to a thick purée. To make a sauce, mix a tablespoon of harissa with 3 tablespoons of oil and 150 ml (¼ pint) water.

A milder version can be made by excluding all the seeds and just crushing the dried soaked skins with the rest of the ingredients.

Makes 150 ml (¼ pint)

Kulikuli
NIGERIA
Peanut balls

This is just one of the many recipes in central Africa which use ground nuts. It makes an excellent light luncheon dish, supper or snack.

450 g (1 lb) peanuts, roasted
50 ml (2 fl oz) water
½ teaspoon salt
oil for frying

If you cannot find dry, roasted peanuts which have not been salted, buy fresh ones and roast them yourself, either in the oven on a baking tray for 15 minutes, or in a dry saucepan and rattle it continually so that the peanuts do not stick. They will be oily and have to have their skins rubbed off.

Grind the peanuts to a powder in a food processor. Add the water and knead into a dough, which is best done with dough hooks in the food processor as this takes the hard work out of it. Add the salt and pour off any excess oil. Take small amounts, roll them into balls and fry until golden.

Makes 12

Gozzoo
INDIA
Spiced tomato sauce

This tomato sauce is wonderfully aromatic and spicy and it makes a very good foil to boiled root vegetables such as sweet potatoes, plantains or parsnips.

85 ml (3 fl oz) corn oil
1 tablespoon mixed mustard seeds
1 tablespoon asafoetida (see page 33)
½ teaspoon cayenne pepper
3 green chillies, seeded and sliced
3 large onions, finely chopped
1 x 400 g (14 oz) can tomatoes, blended with their own liquid
½ teaspoon salt

Heat the oil in a pan and throw in the mustard seeds. Keep a lid on the pan until they have finished popping, then throw in the spices and onions, and cook for a few minutes.

Finally, add the tomatoes and salt. Simmer for 20 minutes until the sauce has reduced a little and thickened.

Makes 600 ml (1 pint)

129

Pakoras
INDIA
Vegetable fritters

This Indian dish is famous all over the world. It is not difficult to make, but be careful not to use too much batter or it will be too heavy. The gram or chick pea flour gives you a light, tasty batter, which is why it is used, but it is sometimes heavier than the extra-light Japanese tempura batter.

Batter:
225 g (8 oz) gram flour (see page 16)
½ teaspoon bicarbonate of soda
½ teaspoon cream of tartar
1 teaspoon sea salt
½ teaspoon cayenne pepper
1 teaspoon garam masala (see page 92)
1 tablespoon dry mint
100 ml (3½ fl oz) water
Filling:
1 large cauliflower, broken up into small florets
corn oil for frying

Mix together the gram flour, raising agents, salt, spices and mint, then gradually add the water to make a paste, beating continuously until you have a thick batter. Let the batter stand for 1 hour, then beat again before using.

Dip the pieces of cauliflower into it so that they are completely covered, then fry in hot oil until they are crisp and brown all over. An economical method of deep frying is to use a wok and to pour oil into the bottom of it to a depth of 5 cm (2 inches).

Serves 4 to 6

Tacos
MEXICO
Stuffed cheese tortillas

Mexico is justly famous for this dish, though you do not often find it made without meat. This is a delicious stuffing.

12 tortillas (see page 62)
corn oil for frying
Stuffing:
4 green chillies, seeded and sliced
1 onion, finely chopped
2 cloves garlic, crushed
225 g (8 oz) feta cheese, crumbled (see page 14)
1 egg, beaten

Mix together all the ingredients for the stuffing, except for the egg. Place one tablespoon of the stuffing on one half of each tortilla, brush the inner surface with beaten egg and press together to form a Cornish pasty shape. To make sure they do not come undone while cooking, fix the ends of the tortillas with cocktail sticks. Pour a little corn oil into a pan and fry the tortillas on each side until they are crisp and golden.

Makes 12

Salsa Verde Cruda
MEXICO
Spiced green sauce

Thousand Island Dressing
AMERICA

The tacos in the previous recipe would be good with this spicy green sauce.

85 ml (3 fl oz) olive oil
225 g (8 oz) fresh green tomatoes, chopped
2 green chillies, seeded and sliced
1 large onion, finely chopped
3 cloves garlic, crushed
1 teaspoon sea salt
generous handful of fresh coriander leaves, chopped

Heat the oil in a pan, throw in the tomatoes, chillies, onion and garlic, and sauté for about 5 minutes. Leave to cool, then blend to a thick purée, adding the salt and coriander leaves towards the end.

Pour into a dish and serve with crudités.

Makes 200 ml (1/3 pint)

I could not have finished this chapter without including one of the most famous salad dressings from America. We are so used to seeing it in commercial bottled form that it is interesting to make it at home. It is so superior.

150 ml (¼ pint) home-made mayonnaise
2½ tablespoons tomato sauce
2 teaspoons chilli sauce
3 black olives, finely chopped
1 tablespoon finely chopped gherkins
1 tablespoon finely chopped chives
1 tablespoon finely chopped parsley
1 teaspoon finely chopped tarragon

In a mixing bowl, pour in the mayonnaise and gently beat in all the other ingredients. Chill before serving with a salad.

Makes 150 ml (¼ pint)

PICKLES

AND CHUTNEYS

*'All culinary tasks should be performed with reverential
love, don't you think so? To say that a cook must
possess the requisite outfit of culinary skill — that is hardly
more than saying that a soldier must appear
in uniform. You can have a bad soldier in uniform.
The true cook must have not only those externals,
but a large dose of worldly experience. He is the perfect blend,
the only perfect blend, of artist and philosopher.
He knows his worth: he holds in his palm
the happiness of mankind, the welfare of generations yet unborn…'*
Norman Douglas, South Wind, *1917*

Pickling is, of course, one of the most ancient ways
of preserving food, along with salting and drying.
The latter was used for fish and meat, while pickling
ensured that the spring and summer gathering of
fruit and vegetables could still be enjoyed in the
winter months. It was then a very valuable method
of preserving the nutritional value of green
vegetables for the months when they could not be
freshly gathered. Some loss of vitamins and
minerals always occurs in pickling, but there is
enough there to make it a good supplement in the
winter months. There are various methods of
pickling — in brine, vinegar, or a mixture of salt and
sugar. The last method was favoured in the East
where the salting of vegetables produced its own
brine and these pickles are often too strong for
western tastes.

Chutneys are an Indian creation which the
English made popular all over the world. These
spicy fruit and vegetable chutneys were traditionally
eaten with rice and curries and it was only the
Anglo-Indians that began using them with their
collation of cold meats. I find these Eastern pickles
and chutneys particularly sensational, which is why
I have collected more of them in this chapter than
from anywhere else in the world.

Elizabethan Pickled Mushrooms
ENGLAND

I enjoyed these pickled mushrooms made by Hilary Spurling from her recipe book of Elinor Fettiplaces. They are a delicious way of having mushrooms throughout the winter, and it is interesting that the Elizabethans flavoured them with ginger and mace.

300 ml (½ pint) sweet white wine
1 tablespoon white peppercorns
25 g (1 oz) ginger root, peeled and sliced
1 blade of mace
85 ml (3 fl oz) water
450g (1 lb) button mushrooms
1 tablespoon sea salt

Pour the wine into a saucepan, and add the peppercorns, ginger, mace and water. Bring to the boil and simmer for 5 minutes. Allow to cool.

Throw the mushrooms and salt into a dry pan and place over a flame, shaking the pan so that the mushrooms do not stick. When they have lost a little of their juice and become tender, leave to cool.

Place in a pickling jar and pour the spiced liquid over them to cover. Seal the jar and keep them for 6 weeks.

Makes 450 g (1 lb)

Mace _The scarlet web-like cover of the nutmeg, with a similar flavour. It is used in pickles and preserves, cheese dishes and mulled wine. It is available ground but has the best flavour when bought whole, which is when it is termed mace._

Sauerkraut
GERMANY
Pickled cabbage

This is perhaps the most famous German dish of all and, while most of us will eat it from a commercial bottle, it is well worth making your own and seeing how superior it is.

2 large white cabbages
50 g (2 oz) sea salt
50 g (2 oz) caraway seeds

Remove the outer leaves and inner stalk of the cabbage. Grate or finely slice it in a food processor. Place the cabbage with a sprinkling of salt and caraway seeds in layers in a large jar, packing it down closely. Leave for 3 months.

Take out a portion of cabbage and rinse the brine away before using it as a pickle or for cooking.

Serves 6 to 8

Sailotyt Sienet
FINLAND
Spicy pickled mushrooms

I make no apologies for another pickled mushroom recipe, because the similarity with the Elizabethan one is striking. It is interesting to see that in Finland they are still making this pickle while we have lost the habit. There are, of course, many pickled mushroom recipes which appear all over central Europe and Scandinavia.

600 ml (1 pint) white wine vinegar
25 g (1 oz) ginger, peeled
1 tablespoon cloves
1 cinnamon stick
1 blade of mace (see page 134)
1 tablespoon sea salt
2 tablespoons sugar
450 g (1 lb) button mushrooms

Heat the vinegar in a pan with the spices, salt and sugar until the latter have dissolved. Allow to cool and fill a large pickling jar with the mushrooms.

Pour over the pickling liquid and seal. Leave for 6 weeks before trying them.

Makes 450 g (1 lb)

Ogurki–Kishone
POLAND
Pickled gherkins

This pickle is exported from Poland in great quantities and is known the world over. The recipe is popular in all the countries of eastern Europe. The gherkins and dill both have a strong clean flavour, which is helped by the use of wine vinegar. The British habit of using malt vinegar tends to destroy all the flavour of the vegetable pickled.

450 g (1 lb) fresh gherkins
1 head of garlic cloves, peeled and sliced
1 tablespoon dill weed (see page 71)
600 ml (1 pint) white wine vinegar
1 tablespoon sea salt

Prick the gherkins with a fork and pack them in a pickling jar with the garlic, sprinkling with dill weed. Bring the vinegar and salt to the boil and, when the salt has dissolved, allow the mixture to cool and pour over the gherkins.

Seal and keep for 6 weeks before opening.

Makes 450 g (1 lb)

Atjar
BOTSWANA
Bean pickles

This is popular in South Africa where it was made by many black cooks. The spices were brought to Africa by the Asians.

1 kg (2 lb) French or runner beans, trimmed
2 tablespoons sea salt
500 ml (18 fl oz) corn oil
1 tablespoon turmeric
1 tablespoon fenugreek
1 tablespoon garam masala (see page 92)
3 green chillies, seeded and chopped

Pour boiling water over the beans and leave for 1 minute. Drain, then sprinkle the salt over them and leave for a few hours. Add a little of the oil to the turmeric, fenugreek and garam masala, and sauté for a moment. Add the remaining oil and gently bring to the boil. Turn off the heat.

Pack the beans into a jar with the green chillies, then pour the oil and spices over them. Allow to cool, then seal with an airtight lid. This will keep happily for several months.

Makes 1 kg (2 lb)

Hot Mint and Coriander Relish
INDIA

This Indian chutney is both hot and aromatic. Limes are often used instead of lemons.

2 green chillies, seeded and sliced
generous handful of coriander leaves
generous handful of mint leaves
zest and juice of 1 lemon
½ teaspoon sea salt
150 ml (¼ pint) natural yoghurt

Place the chillies, coriander and mint in a food processor and blend to a thick mush. Then add the lemon zest and juice, salt and yoghurt. Mix thoroughly.

Serves 6

Sambal Tomat
INDONESIA
Tomato relish

We are all accustomed to tomato sauce but this one, flavoured with limes and hot from cayenne pepper, makes a great change.

3 tablespoons corn oil
450 g (1 lb) tomatoes, peeled and chopped
zest and juice of 2 limes
½ teaspoon cayenne pepper
½ teaspoon sea salt

Heat the oil in a pan and add the tomatoes. Stir and simmer over low heat for about 15 minutes until you have a thick sauce.

Add the lime zest and juice, cayenne and salt, and cook for another 5 minutes. The sauce should be thick enough to spread.

Makes 120 g (4 oz)

Pickled Ginger
THAILAND

We are all familiar with ginger root in syrup but this pickled ginger root in soy flavoured with lemon grass is one of the most delicious pickles in the world.

120 g (4 oz) young ginger root, peeled and thinly sliced
1 teaspoon sea salt
1 teaspoon caster sugar
2 spears lemon grass, sliced (see page 36)
150 ml (¼ pint) light soy sauce

Toss the slices of ginger root in the salt and sugar in a bowl and leave for 24 hours. Place in a pickling jar with the lemon grass and cover with soy sauce. Leave for 1 week.

Makes 120 g (4 oz)

Pickled Garlic
MALAYA

I must confess that, of all vegetables, I am most fond of pickled garlic. An interesting fact about garlic is that it will take on any spice, flavour or colouring that you add to it. Garlic will become yellow if pickled with saffron, or pink if pickled with pimento; here the colour is given by the pink peppercorns and the slices of raw beetroot. Do make sure that you use rice vinegar, which has a very subtle flavour.

6 heads of young garlic
1 teaspoon salt
1 tablespoon caster sugar
600 ml (1 pint) rice vinegar
2 slices raw beetroot
1 tablespoon pink peppercorns
1 tablespoon green peppercorns

Break up the heads of garlic and trim the cloves, but don't bother to peel them. Place in a bowl and blanch with boiling water. Leave for a few minutes, then drain.

Meanwhile, dissolve the salt and sugar in the vinegar, and add the beetroot. Pack a 600 ml (1 pint) jar with the garlic, then add the pink and green peppercorns, and pour over the vinegar. Leave to cool, then seal tightly.

Leave the jar for 6 months before trying the garlic. You will then find that the skins peel off easily.

Fills 600 ml (1 pint) jar

Peking Red and White Cabbage Mould
CHINA

This Chinese pickle is one that has to be eaten as soon as it has been prepared; it is not to be kept. It can be served as part of a first course, or eaten as a relish with a Chinese meal.

1 small red cabbage, grated
1 small white cabbage, grated
4 teaspoons sea salt
4 teaspoons caster sugar
3 tablespoons sesame oil
50 g (2 oz) ginger root, peeled and grated
2 green chillies, thinly sliced
2 tablespoons rice vinegar

Use two bowls and keep the cabbages separate until they are assembled at the end. Sprinkle both bowls of grated cabbage with 2 teaspoons of salt, cover and leave for a few hours. Then pick up handfuls of the cabbage and squeeze it dry. Sprinkle with the sugar.

Heat the sesame oil and cook the ginger and chillies for a moment or two, then divide equally and pour over both bowls of cabbage. Toss both bowls thoroughly and add 1 tablespoon of rice vinegar to each.

Take a pudding basin, place a little white cabbage at the bottom and press it down hard. Add a layer of red cabbage, press carefully, and then another layer of white. Continue in this way until the basin is full. Refrigerate for a day. Unmould on to a plate and cut into portions like a cake.

Serves 6

Kimchi
KOREA
Pickled cabbage

This is one of the most famous pickles in the world and can be eaten either as part of a first course or as a relish later in the meal.

1 head large Chinese leaves, coarsely sliced (see page 116)
2 daikon, coarsely sliced (see page 48)
2 tablespoons salt
50 g (2 oz) ginger root, peeled and chopped
1 head of garlic cloves, chopped
1 tablespoon cayenne pepper
1 tablespoon sugar

Place the coarsely sliced Chinese leaves and daikon or radish in a large mixing bowl and sprinkle with salt. Toss thoroughly so that every piece is covered. Cover the bowl and leave for 24 hours.

The following day, mix together the ginger, garlic, cayenne and sugar. Start filling a large pickling jar with the cabbage and radish, sprinkling on the ginger and garlic mixture as you go. Seal and leave the jar for 1 week before tasting.

Makes 225 g (8 oz)

Aubergine Pickle
SRI LANKA

This is one of those excellent pickles so often made in the East, which has to be eaten there within a week of making. This is not difficult, as it goes well with all sorts of curries or stir fried vegetables and rice. But bottle it here and it will keep for months.

2 medium aubergines, sliced, salted and left for 1 hour
corn oil
6 green chillies, seeded and sliced
1 head of garlic cloves, sliced
1 tablespoon turmeric
1 tablespoon mustard
1 tablespoon fenugreek
1 tablespoon coriander seeds
300 ml (½ pint) cider vinegar

Chop the sliced aubergine, heat the oil and fry the aubergine with the chillies, garlic and spices for a few minutes until the aubergine is just cooked. Add the vinegar and cook for another 2 minutes. Taste to check the saltiness, then bottle and cover with an airtight lid.

Makes 225 g (8 oz)

Nori Relish
JAPAN

Grilled nori has a delicious flavour. This relish can be sprinkled over plain boiled rice or used as a dipping sauce.

3 sheets of nori
50 g (2 oz) sesame seeds, roasted
3 tablespoons rice vinegar
3 tablespoons caster sugar
1 tablespoon salt
2 tablespoons soy sauce

Toast the nori sheets under a grill for a second or two until they become brittle. Place them in a food processor with the sesame seeds, and grind both to a powder. Heat the vinegar with the sugar and salt in it so that they dissolve, and add the soy sauce. Mix everything together to a thin paste.

Makes 25 g (1 oz)

Nori *Cultivated on bamboo frames in shallow water around the coast of Japan, sun-dried on bamboo racks and hand-pressed to form thin sheets, nori is similar to laver. It is much used in Japanese cooking and is usually crumbled over vegetables and savoury dishes as a garnish, or wrapped in whole sheets round grains, vegetables and pickles. It is high in both protein and minerals.*

INDEX

Acknowledgments

One could not write about so many diverse methods of cooking without owing a great deal to some of our great scholars and cookery writers. Of these, paramount among them are Elisabeth Luard for her invaluable *European Peasant Cookery*, Rena Salaman for her books on Greece, Elizabeth Romer for those books on Italy, Claudia Roden whom I have already mentioned, and David Scott who has written so marvellously well on the vegetarian tradition in the Middle East. On India there is Julie Shahni and, of course, Madhur Jaffrey. On China Yan-kit So, and on Japan Lesley Downer.

Photography by IAN O'LEARY

Illustration by ANNE ORMEROD

Home Economy by KERENZA HARRIES

Styling by HILARY GUY

Additional Home Economy by MICHELLE THOMPSON

144